FINDING SCHIFRAH

Publication date: March 2019
ISBN Print: 978-1-7335494-0-0
ISBN eBook: 978-1-7335494-1-7
Library of Congress Control Number: 2018968503

Summary: Born in 1940, Sonja was entrusted into the arms of strangers in the
summer of 1942 when her parents were deported to Auschwitz. Raised by a Christian couple, she emigrated to the United States, graduated from college, married
and raised three children. At age 60, she discovered her Jewish roots with the help
of lifelong friends. Her story raises ageless and universal questions about overcoming childhood trauma and finding oneself.

1. Holocaust 2. World War II 3. Child Survivor 4. The Netherlands
5. The United States 6. Judaism
I *DuBois, Sonja*. II *Finding Schifrah*

Finding Schifrah may be purchased at special quantity discounts for sales promo-
tions, fundraising, or educational purposes for congregations, schools, and univer-
sities. For more information or to have Sonja speak at your event contact Sonja:
ronson1@att.net

Cover Layout and Design: Hanno H. Weitering
Interior Layout and Design: Megan Van Vuren
Editors: Alice-Catherine Carls and Hanno H. Weitering
Publishing Consultant: Mel Cohen of Inspired Authors Press LLC
inspiredauthorspress.com
Publisher: DuBois Press
Printed in the United States of America

*This work depicts actual events in the life of the author as truthfully as recollection
permits and/or can be verified by research.*

Cover: Pre-school photo of Clara van Thijn, circa 1944

FINDING SCHIFRAH

THE JOURNEY OF A
DUTCH HOLOCAUST CHILD SURVIVOR

Sonja DuBois

Edited by
Alice Catherine Carls
Hanno H. Weitering

Table of Contents

This book is dedicated to Mother and Daddy, the parents who gave me life and sacrificed their own life, and to Mom and Pop, the foster parents who kept me alive in spite of danger and nurtured me to become who I am. Without Dolf Henkes and Fie Hartog, two brave people working with the underground, this biography may never have been written.

Acknowledgements

I want to thank the many people who supported, researched, translated, and encouraged me in the writing of my life story.

Gilya, you gave me concrete advice which makes this book wholesome. Janice, you encouraged me to keep working, which obviously we did. Ankie, you helped uncover the mysteries of my life. Without your curiosity and interest, the Belvédère exhibit which chronicled my life would not have occurred. Caro, you have been so supportive, accompanying me to Katendrecht began a new relationship for us and I am honored to call you and Hanno Mishpocha, family. Joop and Linda, you brought me to life in pictures and unearthed precious documents through archives. An amazing exhibit. Esti, the archive material you uncovered answered a myriad of questions explaining the secrecies of my early years. My dear husband Ron, you tirelessly remedied my computer mishaps. More crucial, we are a team determined to support each other in all we do. As always you balance us so well with your patience, always cheering my efforts.

Catherine did we meet by chance or fate? You read my earliest work and encouraged my efforts. You believed that my story could and should be written. You have been my coach and tireless supporter. Hanno, my co-editor who researched, translated, and showed incredible patience spending untold hours editing many chapters. Your energies helped to create my story into a powerful biography.

To all of you who have been my villagers, thank you so very much!

Sonja DuBois
December 7, 2018

The Genealogy of *Finding Schifrah*

> *Do not come barreling into a life full of pain.*
> *Tiptoe around its margins and journey with it into*
> *the unknown. Give it breathing space, let it heal.*
> *Only then can the story be fully told.*
> Alice-Catherine Carls

We all know that it takes a village to raise a child. Lucky is the child who grows up surrounded by loving villagers. These thoughts came to my mind when I heard Sonja's story for the first time while we were riding to the Holocaust Studies Conference held at Middle Tennessee State University in Murfreesboro, Tennessee in the fall of 2013. An instant bond formed between us as I realized that her childhood trauma had failed to diminish her zest for life or imprint bitterness on her soul. On that cold and rainy October day, Sonja was full of life and love as she was sharing her story as a Holocaust child survivor who at 22 months was entrusted to a Dutch Reformed foster family and at age 12 emigrated to the United States. I instinctively became one of the many "villagers" who walked alongside her, and I vowed to help her write her story. The next day, Sonja showed me her scrapbook. It contained outlines of her presentations to middle school and high school students, family photos, letters from Dutch relatives, and the one-page affidavit referring to the events of 30 July 1942 through which she knew that her father had entrusted her "into the arms of strangers." After we returned home, she in East Tennessee, and I in West Tennessee, our email correspondence began. Soon afterwards, Sonja trusted me with becoming her editor. That trust has been the most cherished part of my work.

From the beginning, my role was to facilitate the book. My goal was to collect Sonja's writings and to help her put her story together, insuring that she told it in her own voice. The narrative that she was telling hundreds of audiences during Holocaust remembrance days across East Tennessee, and that she had told to the United States Holocaust Memorial Museum, gave us an initial framework. When she started sending her texts, I was impressed by the richness of her writing register. There were short auto-biographical recollections, the most striking of which were her early childhood memories. There were creative non-fiction pieces about the Holocaust. In the "Dear Alice" letters, Sonja impersonated her mother during the last months preceding her deportation to Auschwitz; she also imagined a postwar reunion with her grandparents who perished in Auschwitz. As post-memory reconstructions, these writings may not fully correspond to historical reality. Nonetheless, their value as literary memorials and as testimonies of self-discovery far outweighed other considerations. Finally, in several pieces in which she used allegories to express her feelings of pain and anguish, Sonja exhibited true literary creativity.

It became quickly clear that no template used to write Holocaust child survivor memoirs would fit, that no scholarly redacting of her story could do justice to her life, and that the interview style with which we had started our work would smother her talent. I chose to work "from inside out," letting her writings guide the chapters' structures and rhythms. This, however, was no small task. Sonja redacted several of the recollections she had told me orally and sent new writings during our two-year dialogue by mean of emails, telephone conversations, and meetings at her home in Knoxville, in Martin, and again in Murfreesboro for the 2015 Middle Tennessee State University Holocaust Studies Conference. We chose as a title *Finding Schifrah*, Schifrah being her registered Jewish name. I was also working to provide historical context to her story. My research efforts, however, yielded limited results, in part because I do not speak Dutch.

This began to change in 2015 when Sonja's Dutch connections were revived under extraordinary circumstances. She finally agreed to request the official documentation pertaining to her adoption proceedings in 1945-1946. After Hanno Weitering translated these documents, Sonja's story matured, revealing deep echoes. The child's feelings are mirrored in the adult woman's gradual discovery of her identity through historical documents. The Dutch villagers who saved the child during the war are echoed by the villagers who helped the adult woman to journey towards self-discovery. As Hanno expanded his historical and genealogical research, he was able to place Sonja's story in historical and social context. Through the ongoing dialogue between herself, Hanno, and me, Sonja shared new details that helped put her story in sharp focus. Thus, the genealogy of this book intimately mirrors her journey towards clarity.

Sonja's story testifies to the difficulty of overcoming a childhood trauma while surrounded by a "conspiracy of silence." Raised a Dutch Reformed girl, she was told the minimum facts about her biological parents and repeatedly urged to move on and live a normal life, thus creating conflicted feelings that explain her delayed recovery of her past. It was like giving her a car key without instructions. Her ambivalent feelings about recovering/forgetting the past are illustrated in the repetitive nature of her initial writings, which were variations on the same events. While we agreed to eliminate these repetitions, they reminded me of the nouveau roman's circular narratives that segue into what is missing. They are recurring throbs of anguish, the soul's demands for an explanation. They are also compulsive fact checking to better circumscribe what is missing.

Sonja's Poetry Book is a powerful witness to her childhood. She received it on her 6th birthday from her foster mother's sister, tante Truus. It is a simple notebook with a plain green cardboard cover. As was the custom in Holland, her foster parents and family decorated the cover and inscribed poems and birthday wishes, limericks, and encouragements to be a good and hardworking girl; they wished for goodness and industry to bring her a "sunny road" in life. This was the symbolic start of her life as Sonja van der Kaden, the daughter of Elisabeth and Willem van der Kaden. Her birthday that year was celebrated for the first time on October 19th, the birth date of Clara Van Thijn, the little girl whom the van der Kadens had saved. Sonja's identity, Clara's birthday. The last entry of the Poetry Book is dated November 29, 1953. It was written in Park Ridge, NJ, by her birth relatives, oom Mark and his second wife tante Joke Spetter. They had traveled from their home in Voorburg near The Hague to Park Ridge,

NJ, to see how Sonja was adjusting to her American life. At the time, Sonja knew them as friends of her foster parents, not as birth relatives. This was normalcy in a twilight zone in which the shadow of her birth parents loomed large.

Sonja's story has drawn a great deal of interest over the years. From Dutch Holocaust survivor Ernest Cassuto's first interest in writing her story in the late 1950s, to hundreds of audiences who have heard it; from her file at the United States Holocaust Memorial Museum in Washington, DC, to her presence in the Tennessee Holocaust Commission's "Living On" exhibit and her participation in the 70th anniversary commemorations of the end of World War II in Rotterdam, her life story strikes a deep chord with audiences of all ages. I witnessed it when Sonja spoke at the University of Tennessee at Martin during Holocaust Week of Remembrance in April 2014. I saw the banners prepared by Lake County Middle School students for her presentation that same week, and I read the letters they sent to her afterwards. These students who came from a wide range of ethnic and socio-economic backgrounds and who live in rural Northwest Tennessee, related instinctively and immediately to the story of a foreign urban toddler plucked from the jaws of death who overcame feelings of abandonment, grief, anger, and anxiety to better affirm love and joy.

Sonja's search for her identity is as complex as life itself. She grew up in an insecure world, at the crossroads of three cultures and two religions. Carrying the proverbial survivor's guilt and struggling against all odds, she nonetheless achieved a state of grace. She accepts that victory does not preclude shadows, that joy exists in a precarious balance with pain, and that life is a series of counterpoints that create rich harmonies. Like a parable, her story is open-ended. Through this opening, enough light comes in to bring peace, enough words to bring healing, and enough strength continue the journey. In this lies the full power and appeal of her story.

Alice-Catherine Carls
Jackson, Tennessee
December 7, 2018

Discovering the Past

When Sonja asked me to translate an old note from Dutch to English, I had only known her casually as one of my wife's many friends from the International Friends Club of East Tennessee. I knew that Sonja was Jewish, that she survived the war in hiding, and that she was trying to learn about her childhood past. I never made an attempt to get involved, before she asked me this small favor. It was August 2016.

The letter documented her parents' final wishes concerning the upbringing of their twenty-two month old daughter Clara van Thijn. They reaffirmed their wishes to a trusted friend, Dolf Henkes, during their final farewell. That meeting took place in the late evening of July 30, 1942. The location was Loods 24, the entrepôt where the Nazis gathered Rotterdam's Jews for deportation to the death camps. Moments later, Maurits and Sophie van Thijn boarded a train. It was the first in a series of forced mass deportations of the Jews from Rotterdam. Several days later, their lives ended in Auschwitz.

Sonja had accumulated many documents from archives in The Netherlands and by glancing through them, I realized I could make a difference. The documents were difficult for her to read, but for someone who still reads and speaks Dutch every day, translating was easy. Places mentioned in the documents were only a stone throw away from the place where I grew up. It all happened twenty years before I was born, close to the place where I was born. Reading the documents became like watching a movie with familiar places in an all too well-known historical setting. It suddenly felt like a moral imperative to help make Clara's story come to life.

Translating turned out to be the least time-consuming task. Finding out 'who is who' and trying to connect the dots required quite a bit of research. Some documents provided direct clues. Others were puzzling and some remained flat-out mysterious. I started searching online for names, using genealogy websites, digitized newspapers through e.g. delpher.nl, obituaries, Jewish heritage websites such as joodsmonument.nl, online data bases such as JewishGen.org and YadVashem.org, national and city archives, cemetery indexes, and last but not least, endless key word entries on internet search engines. Names often enabled me to connect the dots and helped me better understand the course of events leading up to the rescue and adoption of Clara van Thijn. I felt that it was also important to identify the other survivors and victims in Clara's extended family. The genealogy in the back of the book is a chilling reminder of the Nazis' meticulous planning and efficiency in the implementation of their 'final solution'. It also serves to honor the names and legacy of the parents, grandparents, aunts, uncles, cousins, nieces and nephews of Maurits and Sophie van Thijn, who were denied the right to exist.

The fact that Dolf Henkes and Wally Elenbaas were acclaimed artists was a tremendous help in our search for answers. Much has been written and documented about their lives and careers, including their heroic efforts of hiding the most vulnerable from persecution and death. Dolf appears to have been a meticulous note taker and kept his notes until his death in 1989. They are now in the Henkes archive. Had Clara been rescued by an anonymous hero, would we ever have been able to find out what happened?

With the names and dates in hand, it became easier to ask more pointed questions in search for answers. Linda Malherbe, community organizer and project leader at Verhalenhuis (story house) Belvédère in Rotterdam, followed up by finding Clara's adoption record and most importantly, Dolf's eulogy, written by his close friend and witness of the happenings at Loods 24, Rinus Laven. Seventy-five years later we found out, totally unexpectedly, that there was a small silver lining to that otherwise dreadful day. This, perhaps, is the most gratifying and humbling outcome of my involvement with Schifrah's quest. Yet, the research is still far from complete. Many questions remain and answers never seem definitive. Unfortunately, those who could have answered them are no longer with us.

Some of the historical events that were uncovered in the course of this work have made their way into Sonja's memoir. Others are documented in the notes at the end of this book. No doubt, one can fully appreciate Sonja's writing without any reference to the notes. Their purpose, however, is to firmly anchor the literary narrative to factual events, and to help understand the course of Sonja's early life against the emotional backdrop of suffering and war, courage and resilience. General historical contexts, including those surrounding the events at Loods 24, the 1944 Razzia of Rotterdam, and the custody hearings by the commission on war foster children or 'OPK', are easily accessible through reputable websites from, e.g., archives, museums, and Jewish heritage organizations. Whenever possible, I double-checked my information with other independent sources.

It should be kept in mind that historical accounts are only as good as the accuracy of the source materials, and most importantly, that of the story tellers. Not all witness accounts are entirely consistent, which is not a surprise as those accounts first surfaced forty years after the war. In my zeal to fact check Sonja's own accounts, specifically those pertaining to her early childhood years, I found them to be amazingly accurate. This is what also makes her story so compelling and unique.

Hanno H. Weitering
Knoxville, Tennessee
December 7, 2018

Finding Schifrah

Do I remember if my childhood was happy? Did my parents stroll through the parks in Rotterdam? Did they take me to the banks of the Maas River where the water taxis now carry passengers from Katendrecht to the heart of Rotterdam? I, Schifrah, was there. I was less than two years old when the little boat took me and Fie Hartog away. I left my true identity there, almost a lifetime ago.

Feeling safe to be Schifrah has taken the better part of my life. Is it not strange that, even when I wrote in my journal all these years, my true identity was hidden from me. I now know that this was my way of trying to please Mom. Or perhaps this was my method of trying to be good enough. Somehow, I don't think that was ever accomplished. If Mom had preceded Pop in death, would there have been more truth? Mom was definitely the matriarch in the family, and Pop who was loyal followed her lead. Why at some point did I not force them to talk about my life? Everyone has a right to their own identity. Even though they determined who I was, I was yearning to learn who I really am. Not just what one saw on the outside, not just the child who was controlled. Being grateful for having been saved guided every moment of my young life.

At 78 years of age, I am finally complete! Hiding the facts – my being a Jewish toddler in 1942, a part of the Holocaust—did not work. I am a survivor. Thank you to all my villagers for my safety, if not my happiness. Can you see how I have longed to understand my life circumstances? Not knowing often made me angry. But expressing any emotion such as anger, sadness or disappointment, was reprimanded. I was expected to be an even-tempered good little girl. I probably did not measure up, but if I did, I was not rewarded with tenderness. I was discouraged from being introspective and spending time by myself. Even as a teenager, the right to privacy did not belong to me.

Why talk about this after so many years? Because now that I have been liberated, the clouds have cleared and I feel so light. I am finally complete, the puzzle pieces have connected! Each day I marvel at my good fortune. Traveling to Rotterdam for 70th commemoration of World War II and reading the legal Dutch documents pertaining to my adoption made it clear that, even though my birth family failed to gain custody of me, they were truly involved in my life for many years. I just wish that this had been an open relationship. My life would have been different in so many ways. Instead, decisions were made for me. As late as the mid-sixties, when visiting Rotterdam, I did not know of my blood ties with my benefactors. My aunties van Creveld were still alive when we visited Rotterdam in 1965. How special it would have been for the three sister aunties to meet my husband and Monique, our baby daughter. The aunties would have given me the portrait of my maternal grandmother which hung over the fireplace in their Rotterdam apartment. Alas, they had no way to contact me, and their belongings were donated to Jewish agencies.

Knoxville, Tennessee
December 7, 2018

Members of Sonja's birth and foster families are listed in the Genealogy section with book characters indicated in ***bold italic***.

PART ONE

SURVIVING THE WAR

CHAPTER 1

Rescue

Mother and Daddy had just been married when the war began. They lived in the old city of Rotterdam until it was destroyed during the "Rotterdam Blitz" of May 14, 1940. With their apartment destroyed, they settled in an apartment at Vierambachstraat 66a for the remainder of their life in Rotterdam. Beginning in 1941, Jews were fired from their jobs. In May 1942, they were ordered to purchase a Star of David and sew it on their outer clothing. Daddy worked for the Arthur Philip company but was let go in the winter of 1941, after the company was forced to close. The company's reference was very complimentary of his leadership abilities and wished him well, but his employment prospects were slim.

My birth parents were twenty-eight years old when they reported for transport on July 30, 1942. They were sent to Westerbork and subsequently deported to Auschwitz. Mother and Daddy's crime was that they were Jewish. Under Nazi occupation they became undesirables. Within two years of the invasion of the Netherlands by Nazi troops, they became part of the Final Solution, as the calculated murders are called. They lost the right to live, along with six million other Jews.

Dolf Henkes was a Rotterdam visual artist and a trusted friend of my parents. I was told by one of my surviving birth aunts, tante Dien, that daddy purchased one of Dolf's early paintings. Is that what initiated their friendship? Daddy was an amateur painter. It was likely their common interest in art that drew them together. By 1942, Dolf was involved in the Dutch resistance, helping to save Jewish children. He became my first, and one of my most important villagers. Knowing that they were to report for transport on July 30, my parents decided to entrust me to him. Dolf tried to find a hiding place for me in the Achterhoek where farmers often hid Jews and where he had tried to convince my parents to hide with me. There, he left me in the care of a farmer and returned the next day only to find that I was kept in the chicken coop. He took me back home to Katendrecht. He later expressed the anguish of these wandering days in a painting called "Schapedoorn." Its dark colors are indicative of the hopeless mood of those days, and of the frustration he must have felt.

My parents reported on July 30 to Loods 24, a warehouse not far from Katendrecht, where Dolf lived. The warehouse was connected to train tracks and was selected in 1942 as the gathering point for the deportation of the Jews of Rotterdam. My parents were part of the first transport that left Loods 24 on July 30 for Westerbork, a holding camp for Dutch Jews in the northeastern part of the Netherlands, close to the German border.

Meanwhile, Dolf had finally found through the resistance network a family in Schiedam who would take me in. At the last possible minute, on July 30, Dolf, accompanied by his good friend M. P. (Rinus) Laven, sneaked by the guards at Loods 24 to bring my parents the news that I would be safe. They had a very long conversation. Dolf later provided a written testimony:

By order of the father, Mr. Mauritz van Thijn, born on September, 17, 1913, and mother Sophie de Vries, born August 4, 1913, they declared concerning the upbringing of their little daughter Clara van Thijn, born October 9, 1940, that she be given an ordinary upbringing in a Christian family.

This declaration was made by the father at the entrepôt warehouse on or around 29 July, 1942, [at the] Gemeentelijke Handelsinstelling Binnenhaven to the undersigned

R.L.J. Henkes,
born November 14, 1903,
and
Mr. M.P. Laven,
born June 14, 1914.

I often marvel at their bravery. Did the decision to leave their toddler behind come after much discussion between them? Had they heard that the Nazis were killing babies as well? Systematic mass deportations of Amsterdam Jews had started two weeks earlier, so they were aware of the situation. In any case they must have suffered much anxiety when we parted. Was it because I cried that Mother gave me the beads she was wearing, as Marie, Dolf's sister, told me in 1987? Dolf took a big risk to help the disenfranchised. People who were caught hiding or helping Jews during the war could lose their lives. The price was high!

I stayed with Dolf, his sister Marie, and his brother Jan for several days, until I was taken to my foster parents on August 22, 1942. I was only twenty-two months old. Barely a toddler, I was unaware of this dramatic turn of events in my young life. We have all heard it said that it takes a village to raise a child. That has certainly been true in my life; it actually helped to save my life. There were a number of people who were part of the resistance in their own way. There were surely more villagers than I remember.

CHAPTER 2

Mom and Pop

And so the Van der Kadens of Schiedam became my foster parents. I was their only child and was well cared for. *Mom and Pop* were the names I used to call my foster parents. That distinguishes them from my birth parents, Mother and Daddy, whom I do not remember. Mom and Pop were the most important villagers in my life. Mom was born the same year as Mother, 1913. Pop was six years older. There had been a bad miscarriage, and natural children were out of the question. Their need to have a little one to care for was fulfilled when they volunteered to take in a Jewish child.

Mom

Mom's life was long and eventful. While in Holland, she lived in only one city, Schiedam, which neighbors Rotterdam, in the neighborhood called 'de Gorzen' that consisted of working-class people who were born there and died there. She was the middle child, having an older brother, oom Arie, and a younger sister, tante Truus. Mom grew up at Puttershoekschestraat 17. That was a popular place to spread blankets and tea dishes. During the early 1920s, the little girls in that street all played together; the sidewalk was their playground. There were tea parties for dolls with special treats and jump rope, leap frog and marble games. Mom's best friend often provided cookie crumbs to everyone's delight. Her dad ran the bakery on the main street and saved broken cookies for her. When I think of these cookies, the *Jan Hagels*, or "Daddy cookies," that is truly a nostalgia moment for me, because these butter cookies were one of my favorite treats. As a matter of fact I recently answered a call from our granddaughter who asked me to bring this favorite family recipe. Can you image our little ones being excited by such a treat?

I wonder where Mom, tante Truus, and the other girls played on Saturdays when the sidewalks were being scrubbed and the brass door knobs polished. I remember that the street had yellow brick with a herringbone pattern. The girls graduated together into the next phase of their lives. I do not know at what age they learned to knit, but they all did. Each family gave out sock assignments; knee-high dark woolen socks for men and boys were knitted on four very thin needles. Mom also taught Sunday school in her late teens. Her family was very devoutly Reformed Protestant.

How do I know all this? Mom's mother, oma Post came to our apartment every Tuesday when I was growing up and told me the stories. She was also a keeper of the family traditions, so I learned a thing or two from her, even how to knit!

The girls would walk to *het Hoofd*, literally, the Head, which is a popular Maas riverfront site, while knitting all the way with the ball of yarn tucked in their apron pocket. Mom never liked to knit. I cannot imagine why. It is my favorite hobby, even my passion. Oma told me that the same routine took place when she was young. Sometimes a small prize was hidden in the center of the ball. Yarn came in hanks and had to be wound into balls. Did this ploy encourage faster results?

The girls also walked to a park which had many functions. Swings and seesaws may not have been there when Mom was a girl, but I remember them well. As I heard it, it was a place where young couples could find a private place to talk. During the war, tante Truus would take an old gunny sack and a rusty knife and take me along to harvest dandelions to feed grandpa opa Post's rabbits. She would dig them, and I would pick them up, shake off the extra soil, and toss them in the sack.

Although Mom, like almost all girls of that time, did not have a career, I heard that she helped care for ailing children at a sanatorium in a neighboring city. She must have been at least seventeen years old, because there are stories of her fiancé visiting there. They met in pretty characteristic fashion. A group of boys from across town would follow some girls home after evening church service. They would call out to the girls and make a nuisance of themselves. That was their cover to become better acquainted with the ladies. After a few of these encounters, there was some pairing off. Thus began a romance between Willem van der Kaden and Elizabeth Post. Before long there was an understanding between the two, and their relationship was accepted by both sets of parents. They started visiting each other's families and went for walks. Entertainment opportunities were slim, but I did hear about carnivals and ice-skating occasions. Apparently, Pop was quite a show on the ice, which was a popular sport. Their engagement lasted six years; it seems like a very long time, but everyone saved up to purchase their household effects. Buying on credit was not an option, and neither were wedding showers. I did hear that they had an engagement party, but that would not have covered the needs for their new nest. Working in the construction field also proved to have some lean times. So their very important day did not occur until May 6, 1936.

Pop

Pop was born in 1907. He had three sisters and three brothers, all of whom he outlived. Early in life he chose, or perhaps it was determined for him, that he would become a carpenter and cabinet maker. During those years, one began trade school at twelve years of age. Students made their own tools, and we still have some of those handmade instruments. I remember hearing about the early years of his career. Just like everyone else, he rode his bicycle to the construction sites, taking multiple slices of bread and a thermos of tea with him. Keeping enough food for lunch was a challenge. They had an early morning break since the workday ended at 3 p.m. Therefore it was important to exercise self-control. Even though he was a salaried employee, there was no pay when bad weather halted work. The Dutch are a pretty tough lot, but they went through a lot of blackout days. The expression that three seasons can occur in the same day is so true. This situation is usually blamed on the North Sea whose weather pattern has always been a challenge. The work ended at noon on Saturdays, when the end-of-work whistles could be heard all over town. Since Saturday was pay day, Pop often stopped at the butcher who sold horse meat and brought steak home. His youngest sister cooked and served it after she pressed his weekend clothes. He gave her some money for her extra troubles and divided the rest between himself and his parents. It was normal for adult working children to pay for room and board if they lived at their parents' home. Pop's parents had two additional boarders for a while as well. Since girls did not work outside the home, this cash was indeed needed to run large households. The main hobby for most young men at that time was soccer. I believe that Pop's short stature and agility made him a popular team member. Pop talked about his motorcycle as well, although that was a short-lived adventure. When he started dating Mom, she made him give it up. Pop's woodworking skills are still evident in my home. I have a lovely sewing box and picture frames. I often encouraged him to involve himself in such crafts as a hobby after he retired, but he said that his career had been enough for him.

As I understand, many folks of that age group did not have hobbies. They worked hard and did not involve themselves in activities when they came home from work. But they were very social; visiting and having friends or family members drop by was the norm. This may be why there were always cookies in the tin. There were few telephones, so it was a custom to come unannounced. Then there were always the family birthdays when it was necessary to pay a visit. Dropping by was a standard ritual. When folks told us to stop by to see them after we moved to New Jersey, everyone was embarrassed when we did, and we were surprised since we only did what they had asked. But we learned fast and never took their invitation seriously again.

Train and bicycle were the only way folks traveled. Pop's bicycle was his constant companion. He started traveling after he got married. He and Mom married during the Great Depression, when he lost his construction job. Less than a year later, Shell Oil became his employer in the Dutch colony of Curaçao. Although it seems to have been an adventure for him, Mom became extremely forlorn and thus he returned home. Then he worked for a short time at the flooring company where opa Post worked. The only other time he had no job was after the war in 1945. Construction work was slow to restart after the war. In the end, Pop was hired by the Holland America Line as a ship carpenter, thanks to my birth family who had connections in the executive branch of that company. His days of travel and adventure resumed. Much later, when I watched "The Love Boat" television program, I concluded that his employment there had been far from dull.

CHAPTER 3

My First Memories

Precious Items

What do you have in your home that holds a very special memory? Perhaps a trunk in the attic? That is where curiosity seekers discover so many treasures. My special memory is my dress. It hangs in my bedroom closet, covered with a brightly colored pillow case. I do not store it in a plastic bag. It needs to breathe, like it did seventy some years ago when I wore it. This little silk dress was handmade. Did Mother make it? Sometimes it accompanies me to presentations. Most of the time, though, it stays well protected in the closet, for I think only adult audiences can understand the sentimental value of this little treasure.

I was told that the dress was one of the items in my little suitcase that Dolf received from my parents. Perhaps I wore it when Dolf's friend and resistance activist Fie Hartog picked me up in Katendrecht where I had lived with Dolf, his sister Marie and his brother Jan, for a few weeks. I do not remember anything about my stay there. Fie Hartog must have taken me by boat on the Maas River. Then we continued to Ermelo by bus or tram. Mom and Pop were vacationing there in a pension, much like our B&Bs. Can a two-year old really have memories? My first memory in life is our travel on the small boat. The steam from the smokestack was black and smelled bad—odors bring memories of long ago. And there was a small straw suitcase. My second memory is about being diapered. Could I still have been wearing diapers at night? In Holland, not being trained by the age of two was unusual. My bedroom ceiling in Ermelo was made of shiny wood and very tall. I can still see it clearly. I must have lain on the bed while being diapered.

The kitchen in Ermelo was large and had a dark green pump at the sink. That also made an impression on me, since I did not know what it was. I have no idea how long we stayed in Ermelo and no other memory from the place. The first home I stayed at in Schiedam was a second-floor apartment on Kamerlingh Onneslaan 146b. I remember that it had a red door and I will always remember the fragrance of the pipe tobacco from the tobacco shop on the first floor. Potty training likely started when we arrived home. I was awakened by the bright overhead light in the middle of sound sleep to sit on my potty.

Mom saved the items that must have been contained in the little woven straw suitcase. My little blue gingham apron trimmed in red and some baby jewelry are now at the United States Holocaust Memorial Museum along with some additional valuables. An item I was so happy to give away was the medicine spoon, which was filled with cod liver oil. I dreaded that nightly routine. A very unusual item of clothing is among those treasures: a little cotton knitted vest with long garters, a dull rose color. I think that is how little girls secured their stockings. What happened to my other suitcase belongings? Perhaps a favorite toy or a little comfort blankie? Perhaps my new caregivers did not realize the needs of a two-year old orphan.

We then moved to Overschieschestraat 90a, in a second-floor apartment with a view of the Schie river. This must have been a sudden move after the Jewish family who lived across the street was deported. It was important to take every precaution to avoid police searches.

The Parade

In the apartment on Overschieschestraat, the living room had a large picture window. For reasons that I would only understand many years later, I was under no circumstances allowed to be near these windows that overlooked the street below, which led to the train station just out of view. This is where I saw the PARADE. This memory will last the rest of my life. All other parades bring me back to that chilling and dreary procession. I must have been about four years old when I first saw the men shuffling along.

The day I disobeyed and went near the window to see the street below was a dark and bleak afternoon. It must have been near evening for the street lights shone on the cobblestones that were slick with rain drizzle. A drummer followed the columns of men on the street. There was also another sound, perhaps a flute, to keep everyone in step. Five men were marching next to one another in columns that were way too long for me to count. My preschool lessons were coming in handy as I already knew how to count to more than ten.

Their costumes were grungy and they did not resemble those of the happy parades I would see many years later. There were dull brown and grey coats with a variety of head coverings. Some of the boys did not have caps and their blond hair glistened in the evening rain. Not until many years later did I know why the parade took place at the end of the day, and why it was not cancelled due to poor weather. There were no cheering crowds either. Again, it was many years later before I learned that observers always responded with silence to this type of parade. For some of the men, it was the last time they walked the streets of their city. They were sent to an *Arbeitslager* in Germany by foot, riverboat and train. Not all of them would return.

Buttons

A few weeks ago, I spent time thinking about early playthings. Surely mother and daddy sent me off with a favorite toy; if there was a doll or a teddy in my little suitcase, I do not remember it. The most lasting memories are my experiences with buttons. I often visited Pop's relatives with my foster parents. They must not have had grandchildren, or they must have been very poor since I do not remember a toy basket. So, someone must have had the clever idea of sitting me on the floor with a box of used buttons. They were great fun for me and gave the adults time to visit without my interference. I do not remember interacting with adults at all. There was one exception: an old man with a horn as hearing aid. I sat at his feet in a sunny room while he rocked back and forth smoking a skinny white clay pipe, which was popular in the early 1900s. I was initially afraid of him because he shouted when he spoke to me, so I stayed quietly on the floor. But he was a dear. I do not know his name; he must have been the father of the young women who lived there. His horn was fascinating, and he let me put my ear to the other end. There was an echo sound when he spoke. We became friends and he would bend over to admire my sorting activities. That home probably had the best selection of buttons of any home I visited, most likely because one of the aunts was a seamstress. Ladies came to the house to be fitted, their dresses were specially designed and tailor-made. There were also myriads of colored threads on the floor in her studio. Buttons could be sorted in several categories, they could all live together in color families, size or shape. Using a shoelace, I strung together a variety of necklaces. Is this used as an educational activity? Many basic skills can be developed without costly plastic toys. Buttons are a good learning tool and the best part is, kids don't know it. The button box presented itself in other sitting rooms. I wonder if the first box I played with was in Ermelo. All my life, I have kept a button box at my house. But it was not used to entertain my children. It could not compete with Legos, puzzles, and pick-up sticks.

My Five Senses

Which of your five senses are dominant in your life? Have you ever been somewhere and, although it is quite impossible, it feels like you have been in the same situation before? Was it a glimpse of a familiar object, the sound of a tune or perhaps the whisper of a breeze? Perhaps your most prominent sense to recall memory is an odor, just like for me. Today, more than 75 years later, the smell of kerosene gives me sudden headaches. When they occur, I am back in the living room on Overschieschestraat, where the kitchen stove had been moved to the front of the house to heat that room. It was a little round stove with a chimney like an aluminum cylinder. I really don't know how that contraption worked but it released an oppressive odor when simmering food. The other method to slow cook food was in a big box. Pop built a wooden cube from old-looking lumber and lined the inside with hay. A pot was brought to the point of boiling, wrapped in a towel, and placed in this contraption for what seemed a long very time. The result was a perfectly done pan of rice. The box probably had other uses, but I can't remember them.

The smell of shoe polish reminds me of the black boots worn by Nazi soldiers. While it is not an unpleasant odor, I was afraid of those boots that were taller than me. They had taps on the heels. Some members of my family think this is ridiculous, but there will never be black boots in my closet.

The smell of damp wool takes me back to the time when I wore a long heavy cape – a smell like that in a used bookstore. Drizzle comes and goes in Holland, so the cape likely became damp and dried, over and over again. It was difficult to purchase anything in Holland under Nazi occupation. Tante Lena and oom Piet, a policeman, former neighbors of Mom and Pop, had remained close friends, and so it was that I owned a long navy cape. Oom Piet was a very tall man to me. Unless you knew how kind he was, he could be scary, but he sang while he played piano and was always fun to be around. His wife Lena was an excellent seamstress. Out of one of his extra coats, she made this warm piece of clothing for me. The hood of the long cape was lined with bright soft cloth, maybe plaid flannel.

I wore the cape when walking to the aunt and uncle who fed me my daily noontime meals. They were another underground acquaintance that no one questioned. They must have lived close by and they shared their lunch with me. I remember the aunt's name as tante Rie; she was a big soft lady who always gave me a big hug. I do not remember what was served. But it was given by true villagers who helped me survive.

I learned about these villagers sometime after the war, during after-dinner family discussions where I was a fly on the wall. That is how I acquired puzzle pieces of my life. The adults never imagined that I was paying attention and they must have thought that I was completely unaware. But I sensed there was a story yet untold. From these folks, I learned much about our lives during the war. Some of it also finally came to light just before we emigrated to America. By then I was nearly twelve years old.

The Good Doctor

A small child could not survive on the rations from the soup kitchens that operated in Schiedam and other cities. A pediatrician who ignored the rules examined me and produced a birth document with August 22, 1940, exactly two years prior to the day when Mom and Pop took me in. At this time, no one knew my name or age. It was not until after the war that we learned my exact birth date. This good doctor made it possible for me to get food rations.

I was never really hungry, and yet I accepted Pop's portion of soup when he offered it to me. Pop and I shared another secret. Sometimes I helped as he cut sugar beets in strips then cubes to make syrup. We both sneaked a few strips. I did not know why he cooked them, because they tasted fine raw. Pop told me not to tell Mom. I do not think Mom or Pop ever tried to eat tulip bulbs which tasted very bad.

Dusk

I remember how I came to dread the end of the day. Little did I know that the villager who came at dusk helped save my life. I was just a tiny waif in 1942, needing extra nutrients.

Across the Schie from where we lived, there was a pasture with a farm. A woman frequently came across the narrow river from her pasture. She was tall, or she seemed tall to me because I was short. Her hair was fixed in the practical style of the time for older ladies, a gray bun at the nape of her neck. I don't remember much else about her appearance except that she wore the same apron every time. It might have been bright blue with pink and yellow flowers when it was new, but when I saw it, it was sort of grey blue with faded little flowers.

She piloted her vessel manually, propelling it with a long pole. It was unusual, a floating dock which sometimes had some baggage on it as well as the dreaded potion. Farmers had seen their livestock requisitioned by the Nazi forces that occupied Holland. Milk was rarely available.

The mug of milk she brought was from the cow that occasionally grazed on the meadow across the river. It was almost fresh from the cow, and still warm from having been brought to a boil. There was no other way to pasteurize it. A thick skin quickly formed across the top of the rich milk. Since that was the cream and thus the most nutritious part of the milk, it was a shame to waste it. I tried my best to avoid contact with the dreaded skin. Most often my teeth were clamped together as I tried to use them as a barrier. Milk ran on both sides of my mouth, and that was not tolerated. Turning the cup round and round to chase the skin to the other side of the cup did not work either. I was trapped between Mom and the farmer who could not understand this ungrateful little girl.

Late Villagers

It must have been during the spring of 1945. I was scared by the sound of airplanes. We still covered our windows with black-out shades to keep those planes from identifying us as targets. After five years of war folks were not sure if peace was really coming. But these were Allied airplanes that dropped food and aid packages. As I looked out the window, I saw white puffy clouds floating onto the grass.

Since earlier that spring, we had occasionally feasted on white bread and butter. Although I do not remember being hungry, this was a fabulous treat. I think each person had his own half loaf of bread, to either devour at once or hoard some for another time. I probably did not finish my piece at once since I was just a little girl. I will never forget the joy with which I spread the butter thickly enough to see my teeth marks on each bite. When I think of that experience, my mouth says this was better than pound cake. The Swedes, who had sent us flour, knew what was of immediate importance to us: food!

It was some time before the country was again self-sufficient. We all helped with that effort, even the school children. Since fruit trees as well as chestnuts, poplars and oaks had been cut for fire wood, it was now time to reseed. We rose to the challenge of bringing apple and pear pits to class. Our clever instructors devised a contest. All family members, grandparents and friends, brought us their pits in clearly marked matchboxes. All teachers kept count of the collections.

New Uncertainties

After the war, there were new concerns. Members of the Jewish community and surviving relatives were looking for Jewish orphans in order to place them with Jewish families or send them to live in kibbutzes in Israel. My life with Mom and Pop was not assured. A Royal Decree of August 13, 1945 stipulated that Jewish children hidden by gentile foster families would fall under the jurisdiction of the Commission on War Foster Children if no returning parent had informed the Commission of his or her intent to claim the child within one month of the publication of the new law. Mom and Pop had to legalize our situation. I remember climbing steep stairs and facing solemn men in black clothing and hats sitting behind a large table. The staircase was dark. Mom and Pop were appearing before men clad in black. As a result, Mom and Pop were appointed temporary guardians on September 11, 1945 and we had official permission to stay together as a family.

I have often wondered who else was involved in these proceedings. Perhaps my three Jewish great-aunts, Claartje, Esther, and Juul, and another aunt whom I saw regularly after the war, tante Sien, who was the youngest daughter of my grandmother Saartje Spetter.

I have often wondered about Dolf Henkes as well. Apparently, he had remained very interested in my fate. During my preschool years, I remember a teacher handing a picture to someone over the schoolyard fence. Many years later I came to realize that the stranger must have been Dolf and that the teacher handed him my picture. It must have been the one of me pushing the baby carriage that he used forty years later to try and find me. Finding documents has led to another interesting discovery. Until October 1946, my birthday was celebrated on August 22, the day Mom and Pop received me, because they did not know better. After that, they knew my real birthday, October 19.

After these emotions, life on Cartesiusstraat 9a, where we had moved at the end of the war, slowly returned to normal.

PART TWO

GROWING UP

THEY NEVER RETURNED

Even though she is just a little girl, she knows they are talking about her. After all, she is no six-year old dummy! Standing on the street corner, the lady who is pretending to be her mother answers the usual questions. They talk about concentration camps. Are there any survivors? We don't know yet, says the lady. What are survivors, and when are her real Mommy and Daddy coming to take her home?

She wants them to touch her new soft white rabbit fur muff and matching ear muffs. Maybe the people think she can't hear what they are saying because her ears are covered.

CHAPTER 4

My Birth Family

Mother's Family

I remember my great uncle on my mother's side, Carel Drukker. He was married to my mother's aunt, tante Claartje van Creveld. He was a very short and efficient type of person never without a starched collar and non-descript tie. I only knew him as one of my piano teachers. After the war, a lovely upright piano became mine. How did we acquire it? I am certain Mom and Pop did not buy it. Material items were still scarce. Was this a gift from my birth family who wanted to instill in me the love of music? That would explain why oom Carel became my piano teacher.

When I was about nine years old, I was allowed to take the tram by myself to go to Rotterdam for piano lessons. This made me feel all grown up. When I visited the tram station on Cartesiusstraat during the summer of 2015, this memory came back. It was a twenty-minute ride. One of the landmarks was *het witte dorp*, a quaint village of small white stucco homes with red roofs.

After I got off the tram, there was a short walk through the very imposing Heemraadssingel neighborhood. The piano lessons took place in a tall stately building with black lacquered doors adorned with shiny brass decorations and serious-looking door bells. Sometimes I happened to see someone polishing them with the same can of stuff we used at our house. The mail slot in our front door was also made of the same shiny material, probably brass. My lessons were in a small room that did not have any furniture besides a black piano and a couple of chairs. One of those was for the teacher who sat to my right. He would leave the room while I was told to practice the new lesson I was to learn for the following week. When he returned from his cigarette break, I would play it for him to the best of my ability. As I faced him, he would say, "Don't look at me, put your fingers on the keys!" I never became much of a pianist because I failed at putting melody and chords together at the proper intervals. The right-hand and left-hand keys did not work well together. I was eight or nine years old at the time and did not understand the need to practice. The lessons must have been after school, because it was almost dark when I got off the tram and walked the few blocks back to our apartment on Cartesiusstraat.

Shortly after the war, we began visiting the van Creveld aunties. They had survived the war hidden in someone's attic. They were three maiden ladies who lived together in a large apartment in Rotterdam, on Breitnerstraat 85b. They must have been satisfied to see me occasionally. I was always awed by their artwork which appeared to be very modern. They were probably upper class, for they had a chauffeur. It was he who was sent to bring some extra food, likely saved from their food rations. The oldest sister Becky was a skin therapist of some sort. She would take me up to her studio where the smell of rubbing alcohol was strong, it was the same odor that surrounded her. She was not my favorite. Loes was next older and, having no profession, she was in charge of the household. Juul was the artist and I believe she might have been a curator. Somehow it was easy to appreciate her. The home furnishings and artwork were likely of her choosing, quite modern. When we visited, I usually wore one of my lovely dresses sent from California by aunt Alice, my biological father's cousin, although I did not know this detail at the time. There was always a coloring book waiting for me. I must have been excellent at coloring pictures, since a coloring book was provided to keep me occupied during each visit. All three aunts smoked cigarettes secured in elegant holders.

Their meals were tasty. It was hard for them to understand when Mom told them that I was such a poor eater at home. There, I poked at my food, spent many hours at the table trying to clean my plate, and even tried the flushing down the toilet trick, for which I was caught and punished. At the aunties, there was a very large portrait over a fake fireplace. It was either a pencil or a charcoal drawing. With her hair swept up and her severe black clothing, this lady's profile was daunting. She was Roosje van Straaten, the Creveld aunties' mother, and my great-grandmother. This was just another one of the partially overheard conversations that I did not understand. I never went to the aunties alone. When I was sent up to tante Becky, it was so I could not hear tante Juul and Mom discussing me. Whatever was said left me in doubt of who I really was.

Before going to the Creveld aunties, we usually stopped by the house of a man named Boy Frenk. He had survived the war and had two girls, Ruth and Myriam. It was formal, like our visit to the aunties, just like paying your respects. I very much admired the girls' big playroom. I now know that Boy's real name was Salomon. He was the son of mother's aunt Sophia van Creveld and her husband Nathan Salomon Frenk and a successful businessman.

Daddy's Family

I knew this uncle as oom Nap but his name was Noach Van Gelder, and he was married to tante Ro Spetter who was Daddy's aunt. They emigrated to the United States in 1939 with their youngest daughter Henriette. Their oldest daughter, Alice, joined them in early 1940. In 1947, tante Ro and oom Nap visited tante Sien in Rotterdam. They came to see the relatives who had survived. They must have been shocked to learn that I was the only survivor of the van Thijn family. Meeting them was a bit intimidating. It seems they knew me; but they were strangers to me and I again was not told who they were. I did not know if they liked me.

Oom Mark was oom Nap's brother-in-law and tante Ro's brother. He survived the war in hiding. When I first met oom Mark, I was probably about 10 years old, and I was walking home from Beatrix School. A nice-looking car with a man and woman asked me to ride with them. I did not accept rides from strangers and convinced them that I would walk home. When I arrived, the automobile was parked in front of our new apartment building on Lorentzlaan. The only thing I remember from this meeting is that I was praised for adhering to the rules. Who were these people to me anyhow? The next time I saw oom Mark was at a train station, shortly before leaving for the United States.

Tante Sien was the first relative I met from my birth family and the first to reveal my true identity to Mom and Pop. She came to visit us after the end of the war, in 1946. The first time she visited us, she was driven in a long black car chauffeured by a liveried man. I was too young to know the full impact of this visit. Tante Sien brought my birth certificate and other family papers. She also brought a few keepsakes: baby coral jewelry, baby dresses, my Mother's garnet necklace, a demi-tasse service, a silver set of salt and pepper wells, a silver candy dish, and various silver spoons and forks. Mom and Pop gave me these objects in the 1960s, after I was married. Today I have all of them except for those that I donated to the United States Holocaust Memorial Museum. I treasure the delicate demitasse cups and the silver items. My most treasured possession is Mother's garnet necklace.

After tante Sien's initial visit we sometimes went to her house on Wednesday afternoons. We visited her more often than the van Creveld aunties. Since we likely did not have a phone, these visits must have been pre-arranged. Since every acquaintance and friend was called aunt or uncle, I had no clue that some were my birth relatives. I did not know until much later that tante Sien was one of the few family members who survived the war. She lived with her husband oom Wim Landa on de Montignylaan 59 in Hillegersberg, an upper-class neighborhood within the city limits of Rotterdam. He was a Christian and a prosperous businessman. Not much in the memory bank about those visits. Mom and I went by tram. I remember getting car sick, probably because it was before lunch, so my stomach just rolled around giving me nausea. When their youngest daughter Josephiena came home from school, I followed her around. She was a good sport letting a little question box bug her. For me, it was fun being with a teenager.

Somehow the adults always found a way to exclude me from their conversations. I was sent either to the kitchen to visit with the maid or the cook, or to the sun room with a new coloring book. Sliding glass doors kept me from hearing the adults talk. This made me uneasy, because I knew that it was an opportunity for them to discuss me, *het kind*, the child. I was always talked about, but never talked to. Why was everyone so secretive, what was wrong with me? I felt betrayed, guilty.

Oom Wim and tante Sien often gave parties. One was the garden party in honor of oom Nap and tante Ro's visit, in 1947. Oom Nap's hobby was taking moving pictures. I did not know what that meant. When he took out his camera and started filming, I was encouraged to move around. The result was a few seconds of my first and only film appearance, a little star at age seven. Was it at that party that a man took me aside and told me that Mom and Pop were not my real parents? It felt like a bucket of cold water was dumped down my back, I shivered. I told tante Sien what happened, and I understand that this person was permanently uninvited. I still wonder who he was.

At this time in my life, the conspiracy of silence slowly became apparent. I did not learn the answers to some of my questions until decades later; some I will never know. I never knew that tante Sien was one of the very few aunts who survived the war until after her death, just as I was ignorant of the complicated dynamics in my life. After we moved to the United States, we lost track of the van Creveld aunties, and an opportunity to learn about my family vanished. It was only in 2016 that I learned that oom Wim had wanted to become my guardian. This did not materialize and in the end my birth family did abide with the court decision. I am happy to know that they took an interest in my wellbeing and played a role in my life.

There were other family members whom I visited during these years. I never realized that they were my birth relatives. One of them was tante Josephina Spetter who lived in Arnhem. Then there was

Isidor (oom Ies) Spetter who worked for the Holland America Line in a management position. I did not meet him during these years, because he had settled in the United States in the 1910s. He worked there his entire life, rising to a high-ranking position in the accounting department. He stepped into our lives after oom Nap came to Holland in 1947 to visit the surviving Spetter and van Thijn relatives. There was not much work for carpenters after the war; the economic situation was poor, and there was a shortage of wood. Oom Ies brokered a job for Pop with the Holland America Line. Pop started working on their ships probably in or shortly after 1947 and sailed between Rotterdam and Hoboken doing carpentry work.

CHAPTER 5

My Foster Family

Mom's Family

Mom grew up in Puttershoekschestraat where her family lived for a very long time. Her sister Truus Post also lived there until she married oom Frans. Some of the wedding festivities are locked in my memory. It was the first and only time that I rode in a black shiny carriage pulled by two white horses. I think there were several vehicles. There was one for the bridal party and the rest transported the immediate family. We made two stops. The first one was at Schiedam's City Hall, a beautiful and unusual structure. Even though more modern and larger buildings are used for official business, *het stadhuis* is still in use today and thousands of couples have their official wedding photo snapped there after signing the marriage documents. The church is the next stop, with a real sermon as part of the ceremony. I don't remember those details except that as a flower girl I held up the bride's long white train. When we returned home, pictures were taken. All I remember of that occasion is my hand-crocheted baby-blue dress. It was probably tante Truus who made it; it must have been made from some shiny blue silk thread, because it draped nicely. A photo we have at home shows us posing in the middle of the street. Mom could not stop talking about the gross photographic error which has me standing in front of the groom's black pants.

Since oom Frans worked in one of the many distilleries in Schiedam, the party likely lasted long past my bed time. The story goes that in that city infants were washed in the locally produced *jenever* (gin). But I recently found out that it was the new dad who was toasted and doused with the good stuff.

Sneaking the sugared potion from the bottom of ladies' shot glasses was my introduction to adult beverages. It was proper for women to sip the lemon-flavored liquid and, to make it more delectable, they added a demitasse spoon of sugar. No matter how well it was stirred, there was always a residue left for adventurous grandchildren. Those spoons are so delicate that they fit into the liqueur glasses. As everyone sat in a circle in the front parlor, cousin Wim and I played under the large square wooden kitchen table. The tables were covered with tablecloths which hid us very nicely. In the room which was most like the family room, there was a nice big white cloth ironed for a special occasion. The parlor table boasted a cover which looked like a Persian rug. This rug hangs in the front foyer of our home today.

Thinking back, it was a similar cover that saved Pop during the Nazi soldiers' raids. The war machine required more men, and so the Dutch were drafted for labor in German weapons factories. Pop being short would lie on the chairs placed around the rectangular dining table. Fortunately, the hoax worked for him. Later I learned of his other hiding place. It was a practice to keep pigeons indoors in the winter. We had a large cage built into the kitchen wall, little did I know that it had a secret compartment in the back where a short man like Pop could fold into.

Tuesdays were reserved for evening meals with Mom's relatives. Oma Post brought her bread, which she had made and taken to Bram the baker to bake. Tante Truus came, and of course opa Post, who had stopped home after work to change his clothes. I never saw him dressed in anything but a three-piece suit that included a tailored vest and white long-sleeve shirt. Those were tailored for him and I vaguely remember that another uncle from Pop's side of the family, who also tried to teach me to play the piano, was a tailor by profession. On Tuesday evenings, setting the table was usually my job. The menu did not vary much and consisted of bread, cold cuts and sweets. We did not touch our food with anything but knife and fork. Sandwiches were open-faced and consisted of one slice of bread dressed with butter and either ham or cheese, but never both. No one ever listened when I told them not to put butter on my meat sandwich! For seconds or thirds, my favorite was chocolate sprinkles. On such a large piece of bread, you need the butter to hold the sprinkles. It was very special to have opa there, even for a little while. Soon after the dishes were cleared and yet another cup of coffee or tea was served, the guests left. Our apartment building was nearby Truus', so she was walked home. The older folks took the bus across town to Puttershoekschestraat where they still lived.

Opa Post visited often on Saturdays. My bath ritual took place on Fridays or Saturdays. I preferred Fridays because that left Saturdays uninterrupted for my visit with opa. He was my very favorite because he was the only person who invited me to sit on his lap! If he came on Saturday, I was lucky because Saturdays were hair washing days, and often Mom would forget to wash my long black hair. How I hated to have my hair washed in the shallow granite sink. The water was either to cold or too hot. We had to use a special shampoo for dark hair. We were rarely out of the special shampoo! After washing, my hair was smooth, so it was wound in rags to produce those perfect *pijpenkrullen* that were my trademark as long as I can remember. It was not until just before we emigrated that I had a haircut and a perm. You can imagine what naturally wavy hair looked like after such an awful treatment.

Opa and I would sit in an easy chair which was situated under the radio shelf. We listened to the children's radio hour together. There were dramatized stories in which we would be engrossed. Opa would dress down to his suit vest, which smelled of cigar smoke, and I would amuse myself with his watch chain. I will never forget those special moments.

Sundays were often spent at Mom's parents. As a girl of eight in 1948, my memories include learning to be patient. Coffee was served while my grandmother, oma, put the finishing touches on the meal. Potatoes and vegetables were made ready for cooking on Saturday, because working on Sunday was frowned upon. It seemed like I waited for hours for the dishes and naps to be finished after the large meal that was served an hour or two after church. When opa finally awoke, we had our special time. We went to the place where he worked. It was only a few blocks away. On our way, he stopped and dropped off a pan of food. I recall an old man sitting in the back of room where there was no light. Perhaps it was my great grandfather. The little black pan was wrapped in a tea towel. All Dutch households have a set of these black or gray pans and the dishtowels are square. Today I use one just like that.

Perhaps opa was the self-appointed weekend watchman, inspecting stuff, but I don't know what. The factory manufactured flooring; he explained things that I don't remember, but the smell of wood shavings is locked in my memory. We walked around and checked that all doors were locked. When we returned, tea was served with cookies from the tin. Only on birthdays when there were special delicacies, was the tin replaced with a serving dish.

Opa and I were the only two who went to evening church. At evening services, we could sing the songs in the back of the hymnal. These were not psalms set to music, but modern songs not permitted in the formal service. The peppermints he shared with me were a smaller variety than the usual ones. They can't be found today. It was dark out when we returned. I will always remember holding his big callused hand, so reassuring. I knew he loved me.

Knitting

Another ritual took place every Tuesday when I came home from school. Both Mom's sister tante Truus and her mother, oma Post, were sitting by the large picture window. Their knitting needles were clicking. Wool was not easy to find after World War II. I believe it was rationed; it was necessary to have a coupon like the stamps we received for food. It is hard to picture my oma without a grey or black sock in progress. At the time, most men did not wear store-bought socks. Opa wore black ones and oom Frans gray ones. It was understood that each woman in the family had a sock assignment. I remember Mom telling me that growing up all her friends were in the same boat and when they would go for a walk or just visit, the ever-enduring socks would be there as well. Weekdays had a specific number of rows assigned to them, and that number was doubled on Saturday, to make up for Sunday because of course no one labored on Sunday—a brief respite. Sock darning was also an important task. I never saw Mom do any at home because we had oma; but there was often a basket of socks to darn in Mom's lap at tante Sien's.

The summer before second grade, I prepared for the extracurricular activities offered to both girls and boys on Wednesday afternoons. The most popular class was crafts, which included embroidery and knitting. Students had to bring their own supplies, so neighbors and friends hoarded scraps of yarn for me; luckily not all of it was from dark socks. I ended up with salmon-colored cotton yarn. Since no self-respecting grandmother would send her bright and beautiful granddaughter to these lessons as a novice, oma helped birth a knitter. Practice sessions started in earnest that summer. Long thin steel needles no bigger than a size 2 were produced. The salmon-colored cotton yarn, which I learned to dislike with great passion, was cast on for me, and so began my knitting adventure.

I was terribly disappointed not to be reproducing the steady clicking of the needles, which was the familiar sound produced by experienced knitters. There were other difficulties. The stitches did not slide off my needles except at the wrong time and became dropped stitches. How many times did I need correcting! High standards were set outright, and I eventually learned to produce what was expected of me. Even though I did not appreciate my task-mistress' efforts in the 1940s, those early lessons have lasted a lifetime and knitting is my favorite past time. I am Sonja the knitter! I belong to a knitting guild where I learn new techniques, share patterns and ideas; learning continues.

Visiting with my knitting buddies at the Knoxville library kicks every month off on a happy note. Yes, more than sixty years later I still wield the knitting needles. Several times I have taught girls and ladies, hopefully one of them has also become a passionate knitter.

Our Carpenter

Pop started sailing with the Holland America line in the late forties. Most of the trips were on the "New Amsterdam," the company's largest cruise ship. During the spring and summer, he would be home once a month and stayed for a week. During the winter, the voyages were long since that was cruise time. Our apartment complex was always ready for his return since he brought American gifts for everyone. There were treats for me and jewelry for Mom. Nylons as thin as gossamer packed in flat boxes were the favorite. They had a dark seam down the back of the leg. I imagine he could have sold them for a reasonable sum, but they were a gift for tante Truus and Mom. Oma did not wear modern outfits and do I remember her disapproval of such frilly stuff! Large sacks of oranges were quite a treat for many of us kids. Pop also doled out juicy fruit gum. A whole pack of six sticks to a family. Even today when my taste has changed, I always remember fondly those times when I see the bright yellow packages.

Those were fun times for all of us in the Lorentzlaan apartment building since there was always a lot of juicy fruit gum and oranges for us kids, including my neighbor and dear friend Jacques Detiger. His mother, tante Alie, was my contact if Mom and Pop went out in the evening. A colleague of Pop was also a sailor and his wife frequently came with him and visited with Mom in the evening. When both men were home the four of them played canasta at our place. Mom would go to their house when Pop was away. Most often I fell asleep right away and I was no longer scared. One night they all went to the theater after I went to bed. Sometime during the evening, tante Alie banged on the door and awakened me. I would not open the door; that was dangerous. I told her where to find them. Opa van der Kaden was on his deathbed. A few days later, he was the first person I saw as a corpse. I will never forget seeing him as a large waxen doll in pajamas. He was in a coffin at the foot of their bed. Surely oma did not sleep there now? It was a long time before I could erase that sight from my consciousness. I was probably about ten years old then, but I can still picture the scene.

We usually went to pick Pop up when he returned from his ocean voyages. Mom and I would take the tram and return in a taxi. One time he was carrying a wooden box, a cube with holes on all sides. Even though it was not very big, he would not let me carry it. When the three of us were in the back seat of the cab, I asked if this was my surprise. Yes, but don't talk about it until we get home, more suspense! At last we arrived home. It took several trips to drag all the baggage up to our apartment on the third floor. Not until we were ready to unpack his suitcase did he finally say, "there is a pair of monkeys in that box!" They were very small. After he pried the box open, I saw two little gray creatures with big eyes hugging each other. A passenger had brought them aboard on the return trip, but they were confiscated and they ended up in the carpenter's workshop. Pop brought them plenty of fruit and made them comfortable. A new adventure began. I learned that they were creatures from the tropics and needed a warm place. Someone produced a large bird cage which was placed near the stove. Oranges, bananas, and grapes were purchased and soon the little monkeys relaxed in their new surroundings. The neighbor children visited and admired them. They liked to play with shiny objects and this was how we lured them back into their cage. Meanwhile the zoo was called and accepted them eagerly, because there were no varieties like them. To make the separation less painful, we were given zoo passes. We did visit them often in their new home for a whole year.

CHAPTER 6

My Friends

Hospital

Why was I there in the first place? I had open sores on the calves of both my legs that just would not heal. So a stay in the hospital was the only option. The doctor decided to treat them with penicillin, a topical ointment that drew out infection. Sitting with my legs in a deep container of warm water was part of the treatment. Then new ointment and gauze were applied until the next treatment. It was spring time and our beds were rolled out on the patio adjacent to our corridor. There must have been a dozen beds on both sides. With our feet facing out, we snuggled deep under our blankets and watched the weeping willows at the edge of the river sweep gently in the wind. It must have been the time when the floor was cleaned; upon our return, everything had a sharp odor, probably disinfectant.

As a seven-year old my stay was quite an adventure. Together with the other kids in the ward we engaged in interesting activities which helped to pass the very long days. Visiting hours were in the afternoon, I think, but not every day. We were awakened before daylight, why? Same as at home, we all had the awful cod liver oil routine at bedtime. Here however it was stirred into warm milk. I still become nauseous when I recall the fat orange bubbles floating to the top of the cup. This was served in tin cups without a handle, and the cup was as warm as the awful liquid inside. Just like at home, an adult would stay by the bedside until you deposited the empty cup on the nurse's tray.

...r hair were such a craze that they were
...atine and were part of the pediatric nuns'
...ent color for each day, the only one I recall
...One evening we must have been bored and I
...omb my curls. Since there was no water, I repeat-
...omb in the sweet lemonade made of flavored syrup
...r. This particular evening, the staff forgot to remove
...dtime, and so the night nurse did it in a not too a gentle
...whole head had become a sticky mess and the bow was
...o not remember if there were consequences to that prank.
...hospital was a Roman Catholic institution. An embarrassing
...nt occurred on Easter weekend. Some generous soul had fas-
...ed crosses made from pastry and candy to each of our beds. They
...ere shiny braids of bread studded with colorful candies and ribbons
cascading from the circle. This was a Catholic custom with which this
Jewish Christian girl was unfamiliar. Later that day the priest, likely
the hospital chaplain, made rounds and asked if he could pray with
me. Apparently I told him that this was not necessary since I was not
Catholic. Not very polite but entirely innocent. I do not think I was
reprimanded for that particular mishap.

Girlfriends

Willy Vink and I were opposites. That was very obvious even in the
second grade at Beatrix School. Our school was named for the oldest
of the four princesses who eventually became Queen of the Netherlands. Willy had long neat braids with not a hair out of place. I had
black curly hair which would not have been a concern except for the
large bow on top of my head. More like a helicopter than a decoration for a little girl's hair. Unfortunately that was the rage, and I think
mothers tried to outdo each other. Willy had cute little bows at the
end of her braids; they did not fall out like mine did.

We probably were not seatmates. There were two children on each
bench, but teachers were keen on separating friends. This was of course

to keep talkers apart, but apparently it did not work i
told that I would talk to anybody; I was probably repr
daily. Willy said that I broke the silence even while sitting
Mom stormed into school one day when I was in dete
lunch time. She insisted that I stay after school instead, b
not eat well and my lunch hour should not be curtailed.
possible to get the teachers to use their own time after school
have spent a good bit of time in Mr. Luurman, the principal's

There were several siblings at Willy's home. The most unus
was her dad. He worked on embroidery, something that was q
usual in the forties. Today Ron and I still have one of his pro,
cross-stitched *Schellekoord* (bell-pull) showing a variety of wina
each indigenous to their village. We received it as a wedding gift
are still enjoying it.

How did we keep ourselves entertained? We did play marbles a
often played for keeps. Stilts were also a favorite item since Will
older brothers could make them, and thus they did not have to b
purchased in a store. Playing inside was another story. We had a big
box of broken crayons that Willy shared with her younger sister. On
Saturdays, when opa visited, Willy and I listened to the children's story
hour on the radio at my house.

I only remember two girlfriends. Mom generally would not let me
play after school, but Willy and Nelly were the exceptions. We all lived
about the same distance from school. Nelly had an older sister who
had us perform her plays. I still have one of her costumes, a Dutch hat
made from crepe paper. We celebrated Mom and Pop's twelve-and-a-
half-year wedding anniversary with Nelly's sister as the playwright. I
think that one of her plays included a dance. She took a funny photograph of it which produces a nostalgic memory each time I look at it.
Nelly died from kidney disease after we emigrated.

Just like everyone who knew me, Willy was told to not ever let me
know that I was a Jewish girl. How were they made aware? Was it a
shame to be Jewish? In any case, my friendships were very restricted!

nly many years later did Willy have the courage to disregard that
ict. That was in 1987, when she sent me the newspaper article with
olf Henkes' interview, "What happened to Claartje?" So it took
bout 40 years for her to break the silence and become my first connection to my past. She was the first person who painstakingly worked
on my genealogy and put me in touch with Dolf. We remain friends
to this day. Snail mail may be old-fashioned but I still anticipate her
Christmas messages which are usually a sample of her delicate art
work. I have saved them all!

Jacques

Our apartment building on Lorentzlaan was brand new. We had
moved there in 1949 and lived on the top floor, probably the fourth
floor. Jacques Detiger's apartment was a walk-up, so he was my down-
stairs neighbor. I had a crush on him. Our parents were close friends
and that must be why we were often invited to watch television with
them. His parents had the first set in our building. It was a first-time
experience for me. His parents sat on the sofa facing the magic box.
Jacques' sister Hennie, Jacques and I sat on the floor, staring at the
round screen with the clock that counted the minutes before the news.
I don't remember other shows. Neither radio nor television was regular
entertainment for us then.

It was a couple of years later, when I was eleven years old, that I
learned to use my girlish ways. One of my least favorite chores was to
go down to the basement. There was a screened-off and locked coal
bin and I was to fill the carrier and haul it back upstairs. The lighting
system filled me with trepidation. It was on a timer and would leave
me in complete darkness between floors. At first, I reasoned this out.
If I left my bucket on a step and ran up to the next floor, pushed the
switch and returned where I came from, I could make it to that spot
without losing light. It seemed a futile chore since I would come back
with half a load of coal. I worked out an easier method. Jacques usually came home sometime in the early evening. He was strong and

handsome. Just right for this job, and even though I had to suffer his superior attitude, he was a great help. Timing was everything! I would be struggling up the first flight of stairs when he came through the front door. He would lift the bucket and mock me for filling it only half full. So we went back to the bin to fill the bucket to the very top, and he carried it to my destination. I never realized until much later that he saw through my scam.

Jacques stayed in close relationship with us after we emigrated to the U.S. He visited and even lived with us for a short while in 1957, then moved to New York. We dated during that time. He often came to Sunday dinner and we always took a walk, sometimes holding hands. He eventually moved back to Holland. We told him to go to the Holland America Line and to look up Ies Spetter, who gave him his first job. He has since built a prosperous business in the shipping industry. Each Christmas he sent out beautiful artist calendars to Mom. After she died, I wrote the company and told them that the gift was no longer necessary. It was then that Jacques and I renewed our relationship. He called often. He told me about the war: how Jewish classmates would disappear from school without explanation, how he knew that I was Jewish and was sworn to silence, just like Willy. Even though he is not Jewish, it was from him that I received several Jewish books. He also sent me the Dolf Henkes art book which includes the Schapedoorn landscape. When we visited in 2015 at the Belvédère House in Rotterdam, he told me that mine was not a one-way crush back then, and we talked about what might have been!

The Care Packages

After the war, we started receiving packages from America. They were sent by my mother's cousin aunt Alice from her home in Oakland, California. My cousin Jocelyn was just a little older than me and her slightly used clothing made me the best-dressed third grader. A lovely, maybe even professionally made photo with me sitting at the piano pretending to play, has survived the lessons. I wore one of those lovely dresses when visiting the van Creveld aunties. Did little girls in California also wear huge bows in their hair? Perhaps Mom just matched one of these with the American outfits.

The packages also contained snacks. Perhaps that was when I tasted my first peanut butter sandwich, which I ate as an open-faced sandwich, with fork and knife, and without jam—we did not eat peanut butter with jam.

The packages also contained swimming suits. Whatever day it was for the terrible swimming lessons, I dreaded this activity from the moment I stepped off the bus. I had my own bus card, probably it was punched by the conductor. The chlorine vapors assailed me as soon as I opened the heavy glass door. The whole place was steamed up and voices bounced off the walls, creating an unbelievable racket. I received a key and was off to the locker room that had wooden slats all over the floor. I wore one of cousin Jocelyn's swimsuits, they were very colorful. The cold shower was mandatory, and so began my least favorite hour of the week. It was not until you submerged yourself in the water, which was not very cold, that the corks were thrown in as floating devices. The instructor would use a long pole with a hook to coach one around the edge of the pool. That must have been to learn the proper leg strokes. What happened between that activity and jumping off the high dive is a blur. To graduate, everyone without exception had to stand on a very high platform, look straight ahead and take the plunge. Since I did earn a certificate, I must have completed that feat, but that has been permanently erased from the memory bank. Coming from the pool to the locker room, I once again walked through a curtain of cold shower water. This time it was more pleasant, for this chaos was over for another week. It was not until later, when I was away from that dreadful pool, that I learned to swim well enough to save myself from drowning.

CHAPTER 7

Going to America

Life Changes

Soon again, my world changed. Mom and Pop planned a new life in a new country. Why? There were no new birth relatives to claim me. I had lost both my parents, all four grandparents, all my uncles and aunts, and all my cousins. There were no known de Vries or van Thijn survivors. The remaining great aunts and uncles and cousins were distant ones. My great-aunts Rebecca, Claartje, Esther, Loes and Juul van Creveld survived the war and (with the exception of Esther) lived on for many years. Of the Spetter family members, four out of nine survived: tante Josephina, tante Sientje, tante Ro, and oom Mark.

Perhaps Mom was afraid that I would start asking about my Jewish roots and maybe lose my Christianity or be overwhelmed by the enormity of the losses my birth family suffered? Was that why she chose to make a complete break, even though emigrating represented a huge sacrifice for her? The year 1952 was a year of emigration for many Dutch Jews, such as Ernest Cassuto, author of the book *The Last Jew of Rotterdam*, and also for many Dutch people. Maybe the US immigration rules loosened. Had Pop been given a new job opportunity? Was it thought a better future could be built for me in the United States?

Oom Nap and tante Ro van Gelder already decided before the war that they had no future on the old continent and emigrated to the United States in 1939. Oom Ies Spetter, who worked for the Holland

America line as a high ranking executive, had already made that move in the 1910s and may have helped the van Gelders settle in New Jersey. Oom Nap and tante Ro became our sponsors and initial hosts when we arrived at the Hoboken piers. We lived with them for a short time until they found us a temporary home. All this behind-the-scenes family support and encouragement for *het kind*, as I was referred to, took place without my knowledge.

Packing

In the summer of 1952, tante Truus helped us pack. She brought an empty little suitcase with her; it was often bulging when she left. She became the depository for all the things we could not take with us. It seemed that she came and went constantly that summer. Friday was one of the days I was sure to see her, because that was cleaning day. Since her apartment was right around the block and it was small, she had time to help us after doing her chores.

We were leaving not just the apartment, the street, or the city, but even our country! That was called emigrating. Even though many families were doing just that, I did not know any other kids who were in my situation. I was ready for an adventure, but it was kind of scary. Decisions on what to take and what to leave were made on an hourly basis. I thought that a good way to keep out of the way was to start a diary. Faithfully, I wrote at least one paragraph a day for nearly two weeks. Later, the notebook went into the leave-behind pile. I did not regret that decision. I did not start recording my thoughts again until twelve years later. Today, my filled diary books are stored on a high shelf in my bedroom closet.

On Saturdays we went into the big city of Rotterdam. That is where all the department stores were located. We purchased my going-away wardrobe. I don't remember shopping for clothes, but I do recall some of the outfits we purchased. There were cordovan shoes and beige knee socks, a yellow dress with white polka dots and a bow on either side of the waist. Practical shoes, pants and dresses. There was a pair of corduroy pants which hung in the very back of my closet until I had outgrown them. I wore the raincoat often. It had a soft furry lining and doubled as a winter coat. To wear new clothes was important to my folks who wanted me to be well-dressed, even if the choices were peculiar in my new environment. Why did we not purchase new clothes in the U.S.A so that I could look like the rest of kids?

Discovering Clara

Shortly before my twelfth birthday, I learned to write my name! That would not be too unusual except that Mom and Pop finally told me what it was: Clara!! For years I pretended to be ignorant of the fact that Mom and Pop were not my real parents. There had been hints, for sure. I remembered the street corner conversations between Mom and neighbors. The answers to the questions were always "we haven't heard yet", spoken in a hushed voice so I would not hear. The adults presumed that I could not hear or did not listen, but I soon understood they were discussing me. Now all the questions came back. Why had my mother and daddy abandoned me? Couldn't they understand that I worried, wondering why they had left me? I had suppressed these questions, really trying to be a good girl for Mom and Pop.

On a Wednesday after school, in the fall of 1952, while we were making preparations to go to America, the truth was finally spoken. "Your parents died in a concentration camp during the war. Your name was Clara Van Thijn and you need to practice copying these words because you need to sign your passport."

One of my strong memories of that day is a photo of Mau and Sophie van Thijn, my real parents. They showed it to me that afternoon. They held it up as they sat across from me in the living room. I could only see mother and daddy from a distance. I noticed that daddy had a strangely-shaped ear. That photo must have been one of the items brought by tante Sien to Mom and Pop shortly after the war. I never saw it again, and this has bothered me all my life. When Mom moved into a nursing home and left personal belongings behind, I searched for it in vain. Was it destroyed, and if so, why?

On that afternoon in 1952, when Mom and Pop told me that mother and daddy were Jewish, that did not really register in my mind. Such huge life-changing information was thrown at me without concern for my feelings. At that time, I truly did not know what it meant to be Jewish. "You were too young to know your parents and you don't remember them, do you? That is why you should not think about the past at all. You belong to us now, we protected you and made you our child, Sonja." During the brief explanation, I remember feeling cold chills running up my back. It was the same feeling that I experienced in 1947 when I learned at tante Sien's party that my parents had died. Yet I acted in a very placid manner. Instinctively I knew not to speak up. Even though I did not know much about the Holocaust, I had long felt that Mom and Pop were not my birth parents. At twelve years of age, I should have been inquisitive but felt intimidated. And I was in fact being told not to consider myself a Holocaust survivor. Since I did not remember physical suffering, I must not be a Holocaust survivor. Emotional pain did not count, especially for a child. I was fortunate to be alive, so why bother with the past, did it even happen? Both my body and soul had been saved when Mom and Pop made me a Christian. Perhaps that is why they took me in? I had often been told that I was not grateful, so I never really felt good enough, no matter how hard I tried to be all that was expected. To further earn their approval, I did not reveal my suspicions about Clara in 1952.

I was nearly twelve, I had just discovered my new identity, and I was about to leave everything and everyone I had known all my life.

Right: My aunt Alida (Alice) van Gelder with Daddy around 1930.

Below: Mother and daddy at the wedding of Alida van Gelder and Shlomo (Steven) Shulster on February 2, 1938. The image was captured from film and is the only picture I have of my parents. Aunt Alice gave it to me when we met in Israel in 2000.

Toelichting zie keerzijde

Aanmeldingsformulier voor één persoon,
die geheel of gedeeltelijk van joodschen bloede is (Verordening 6/1941)
Invullen met schrijfmachine of met inkt in blokletters

1.	Geslachtsnaam: (een vrouw vult hier alléén haar meisjesnaam in) Voornamen: (alle voluit)	**Van Thijn** **Clara**
2.	Geboorteplaats: (gemeente) Datum van geboorte: (dag, maand en jaar)	**Rotterdam** **19 October 1940**
3.	Woon- of verblijfplaats: Straat en huisnummer: Laatste woonplaats in het Groot-Duitsche Rijk (met inbegrip van het Protectoraat Bohemen en Moravië) of van het Gouvernement-Generaal voor het bezette Poolsche gebied: (invullen voor hen, die na 30 Januari 1933 in Nederland genaturaliseerd zijn)	**Rotterdam (W)** **Vierambachtsstraat 66 A**
4.	Nationaliteit: en Eventueele vroegere nationaliteiten:	**Nederlandsche** **geene**
5.	Kerkelijke gezindte:	**Ned.Israel.Gemeente**
6.	Beroep of werkzaamheid: (duidelijk omschrijven)	**geen beroep**
7.	Ongehuwd, gehuwd, weduwnaar, weduwe of gescheiden van: (naam en voornamen van echtgenoot(e) of gewezen echtgenoot(e) voluit)	gehuwd met: **ongehuwd** weduwnaar van: weduwe gescheiden van:
8.	De onder 1 vermelde persoon: a. behoorde op 9 Mei 1940 tot de joodsch-kerkelijke gemeente b. is na dien datum daarin opgenomen c. was op 9 Mei 1940 met een jood gehuwd d. is na dien datum met een jood in het huwelijk getreden	ja/neen ja/neen ja/neen ja/neen
9.	Hoeveel joodsche grootouders in den zin van artikel 2 der verordening (zie keerzijde): (invullen in letters)	**vier**
10.	Opmerkingen:	

Niet zelf invullen	Par. ambt.	Ondergeteekende verklaart het vorenstaande naar waarheid te hebben ingevuld.
Ingekomen d.d. f 1,— { voldaan / niet voldaan Vermindering Reden: tot een bedrag van f. } Vrijstelling: Vergeleken met en aanduiding geplaatst op: Persoonskaart Verblijfregister Sign. aangebracht Bew. v. aanmelding afgegeven d.d. Verzonden aan } Hoofd R. Insp. { d.d. Ontvangen door } Bevolk. reg. { d.d. N.S.18323		Gemeente **Rotterdam** **12 Februari** 1941 (handteekening aanmeldingsplichtige) Uitgegeven met toestemming van het hoofd der Rijksinspectie van de bevolkingsregisters beschikking dd. 31 Januari 1941 nr. 5

My registration form with the occupying authorities. Daddy filled this out on February 12, 1941, one month after it became mandatory. It states that I have four Jewish grandparents, meaning that I was considered fully Jewish and would be among the first to be targeted for deportation to the death camps.

NEDERLANDSCH ISRAËLIETISCHE GEMEENTE
TE ROTTERDAM

TELEFOON 48940
POSTGIRO 65490

Rotterdam, den 11 Juni 1941.
Ged. Botersloot 73

No. ....

Nota: Bij de aanhaling dezes dit nummer
en den datum te vermelden.

       Naar aanleiding van Uw gesprek hedenmorgen met den heer
Jacobs deel ik U mede,dat ik Uw dochtertje destijds ingeschreven heb
zoowel op de kaart van den Burgelijken Stand als in het geboorte-
register.In dit register staat tevens haar Joodsche naam Schifrah
vermeld.

                               Hoogachtend,

Den Heer M.van Thijn
Vierambachtsstraat 66a
Alhier.

*This letter from the Jewish Congregation in Rotterdam to Daddy dated June 11, 1941
confirms that I was registered in the city's birth register. It gives my Jewish name,
Schifrah. Daddy had spoken to them that very morning. The quick turnaround sug-
gests some urgency. Roundup of Jews had begun. Did Daddy request this letter so that
I would have proof that I am Jewish? Was he starting to make plans for me?*

A R T H U R   P H I L I P   &   C O.   =   R O T T E R D A M . -

31 Januari 1941 . -

G E T U I G S C H R I F T . -

Tengevolge van de opheffing van ons bedrijf in verband met de veranderde
omstandigheden, zien wij ons genoodzaakt onzen procuratie-houder den

heer   M. van T h i j n

uit onze dienst te ontslaan. -
Genoemde heer was vanaf 2 October 1939 tot en met heden in ons bedrijf werk-
zaam.-
De heer Van Thijn leidde de binnen- & buitenlandsche correspondentie; boven-
dien is hij goed op de hoogte met banktechnische aangelegenheden en behandel-
de hij in het bijzonder de afwikkeling der overzeesche transacties.-

Wij betreuren het zeer, dat wij den heer Van Thijn, die bijzondere capaci-
teiten bezit om een leidende positie in te nemen en groot vertrouwen bij ons
genoten heeft, door de omstandigheden moeten ontslaan.- Wij kunnen hem
daarom steeds aanbevelen en onze beste wenschen begeleiden den heer
Van Thijn voor de toekomst.-

Rotterdam, 31 Januari 1941

Mo/-

*Daddy's certificate and reference letter from Arthur Philip & Co. The letter is very com-
plimentary of Daddy's job skills and leadership attributes and wishes him the best.*

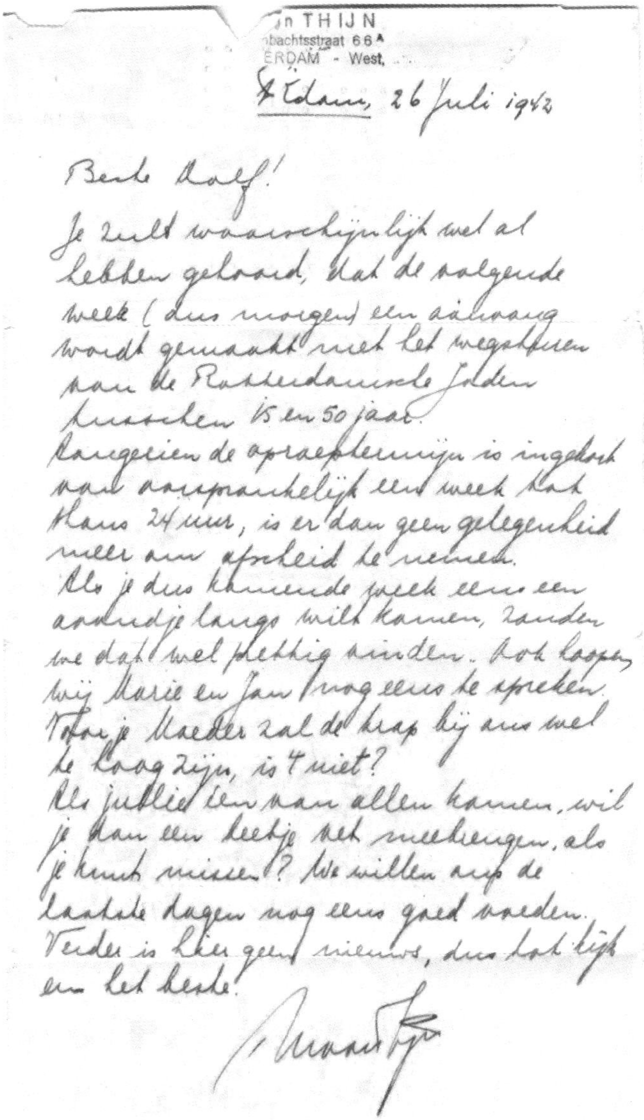

THIJN
bachtsstraat 66ᴬ
ERDAM - West,

R'dam, 26 Juli 1942

Beste Dolf!

[Handwritten letter in Dutch cursive]

Daddy's letter to his friend Dolf Henkes from July 26, 1942. He is telling Dolf that
they will be deported within the next few days. He asks Dolf, Marie and Jan to stop
by for a final farewell. Did they meet before July 30 and did Mother and Daddy hand
me over at that time?

Dolf Henkes Archives. © Joop Reijngoud (Verhalenhuis Belvédère) by courtesy of RCE
Rijksdienst voor het Cultureel Erfgoed.

Affidavid by Dolf Henkes and Rinus Laven, stating it was my parents' wish that I be raised in an ordinary Christian family. The handwriting is Dolf's.

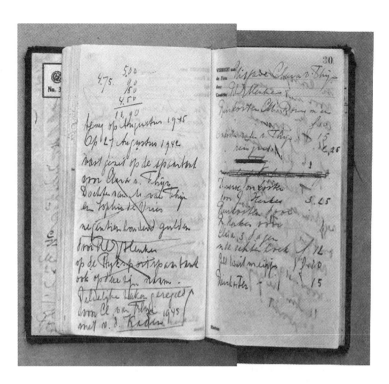

Pages above from Dolf's notebook list some of the expenses of my three-day trip to the Achterhoek. He deposited 1900 guilders at the bank in 1942 and "arranged money matters" with Pop in 1945.

Right: Daddy bought artwork from Dolf, such as a painting of the "Groote Schouwburg".

Dolf Henkes Archives. © Joop Reijngoud (Verhalenhuis Belvédère) by courtesy of RCE Rijksdienst voor het Cultureel Erfgoed.

This little dress was in the little suitcase that my parents gave to Dolf in July 1942.

I still keep it in my closet at home. It is one of the treasures that connect me to the past.

This is Mother's necklace with the Jerusalem beads. She put it around my neck when we parted.

Photos © Linda Malherbe (Verhalenhuis Belvédère)

Until early 2001, I did not know that the painting that hangs in my living room was Daddy's work. It looks like a forest weathering a storm, with a faint sunny path leading to safety.

Photo © Linda Malherbe (Verhalenhuis Belvédère)

Fie Hartog took me under her wings and brought me to Mom and Pop in August 1942. She risked her life for me. Fie testified on my behalf to the OPK in 1945. Shortly thereafter, she died after a brief illness.

© Esther Elenbaas-Hartog, ca. 1935, in courtesy of RKD Nederlands Instituut voor Kunstgeschiedenis

Family pictures with Mom and Pop. This must have been shortly after the war as Pop is wearing his uniform of the citizens' militia.

Tante Sientje Spetter was the youngest sister of my grandmother Saartje Spetter. She was married to oom Wim Landa. After the war, she brought Mom and Pop several important documents and valuables that belonged to my parents. I believe she and oom Wim provided some financial support for my upbringing.

Tante Sien brought a necklace that belonged to my mother. It is very special to me and I only wear it on special occasions.

Wedding of oom Frans and tante Truus shortly after the war. I am in the middle, standing in front of the groom's black pants

I took piano lessions with oom Carel Drukker. Did my Jewish relatives buy the piano for me?

With my lifelong friend Willy Vink around 1952

My 1962 wedding to Ron.
With Mom and Pop.

Dolf gave me this picture of him working in his studio when I visited him in 1987.

This picture was taken during our 2000 trip to Israel. From left to right: Beverly, Ron, Jocelyn, and aunt Alice

Sifra Dasberg and I at the 2015 exhibition "Het verhaal van Sifra & The Story of Schifrah" at Verhalenhuis Belvédère in Rotterdam.

With Linda Malherbe at the Loods 24 Childrens' Monument. The names of 686 deported Jewish children age 12 and below are engraved in the metal table. A small section of the wall enclosing the railway entrepôt is left standing in the back.

Photos © Joop Reijngoud (Verhalenhuis Belvédère)

PART THREE

TEENAGE YEARS

CHAPTER 8

Settling in New Jersey

Arriving at Hoboken Pier

We sailed from the Netherlands on October 4, 1952 on the S.S. Rijndam. I became seasick as soon as we crossed the English Channel, which is not uncommon. After several meals, the tablecloths were sprinkled with water. That was the precaution taken when the captain knew that the boat was going to rock. That way, the glasses stayed in place. Next, the edges of the dining tables were raised. Only seasoned passengers were still hungry and prevailed through dinner. I spent the majority of the voyage in a deck chair covered with lovely plaid blankets. I was at my post first thing in the morning before the first breakfast was served. Kind people would come and gaze at me, often bringing apples, crackers or other goodies which they thought would make me feel better. I collected quite a stash.

Our voyage became somewhat turbulent and we did have a lifeboat drill. Thinking back to that time, there must have been some anxiety, but I was too sick to care. The water was gray and foaming. Pop had sailed the ocean as an employee of the Holland America line prior to our emigration. He used to tell us how powerful the waves could be. He said that even a big luxury liner would be like a matchbox on the waves.

After twelve days which seemed like at least a month, at last, I saw the famous Statue of Liberty, which meant that I could finally step onto solid ground! It was October 13. Hoboken was our port of entry and all the passengers were at the railing, looking for a familiar face. In our case, only Pop would know if our sponsors were among the many people waving and shouting to their loved ones. I do not remember many of the activities of the day, except that there were huge letters hanging in the baggage area. We looked for the letter K for van der Kaden and waited in a long line. That is how we passed through customs.

The First Month

My aunt Alice's parents, oom Nap and tante Ro van Gelder lived on 8, 6th Street in Park Ridge, New Jersey. They were our sponsors and became our initial hosts when we arrived at the Hoboken piers. I do not recall the trip from Hoboken to Park Ridge, New Jersey. And I have no memory of the first few days at our sponsors' home. As usual I called them aunt and uncle, not knowing that they were my biological relatives. We lived with them for a short time until they found us a temporary home.

After just a few days at their house, tante Ro and oom Nap arranged for us to stay at the Braun's summer day camp. Located in a spacious wooded area, the camp included a cottage. Since the camp was deserted in September, we lived in the caretaker's cabin, another sign that the van Gelders were well connected. It was a unique location, a good base for us after the many changes that had just taken place. I will always remember the screen door that slammed shut when one forgot to hang on to it, the dark, chipped linoleum with throw rugs that always slid around, and the very cold bedroom with bunk beds. The thin summer blankets did not alleviate the chills. We missed our heavy woolen blankets. They were in the crate which had not yet arrived and that contained all the household goods from our home in Holland. In the large live-in kitchen, a cooking stove provided heat only for the immediate area. I loved to stand in front of the glowing stove as a new day dawned. I do not remember if we fed it coal or wood. It was a big black object near which we ate breakfast. Since cold cereal was unknown to us, Pop poured warm milk on his rice puffs, making a nice mush. In the evening, we sometimes visited with tante Ro and oom Nap at their home and walked about half an hour back to the cabin. We had a flashlight to keep us from tripping on the uneven sidewalks. When we neared the cabin's clearing, the streetlights glowed.

It was at the Braun camp that I celebrated my 12th birthday. My first American birthday, shortly after our arrival. In Holland, family gathered together for coffee and baked goods, and it was mostly another opportunity for the grownups to visit with each other. This American birthday party was a new experience. It was all about me, with candles to blow out on a cake, balloons and little party bags, games and songs that made this an unforgettable experience. I must have received gifts, but I do not remember any. It had begun to snow earlier that day, as I walked home from school. This bit of white October wonderland was unusual for New Jersey, even if they had long winters.

Our New Home

We moved into a two-bedroom house in Park Ridge on Tuxedo Avenue, about one month after we arrived in the United States. We initially rented it, then eventually owned it. I always thought of our two-story cedar-shingled dwelling as the house from the Hansel and Gretel fairy tale. The crate we had packed in Holland arrived in early November. It contained all the things from home which included bedroom, dining room, and kitchen furniture. Also bedding, kitchen paraphernalia, a good bit of the famous Delft Blue china, and of course the coveted wool blankets. My Murphy wall bed and bookcase went upstairs to my bedroom. My friends always wondered where I slept: they had never seen a bed that folded into the wall. Since mine was a small room, this was a perfect solution.

The crate was as big as a house in my estimation; it would have made a grand playhouse. But it became Mom's security check for returning home. She made up her mind days after our arrival that this move was a mistake. Why did we need to leave Holland? Mom mourned leaving her parents and was never happy with her new life. Was I responsible? I was often told that this had all been done for me!

Adjusting

Learning English was difficult for Mom and Pop although Mom threw herself right into it. Starting a sentence in English, she sometimes ended it in Dutch. Pop worked in a cabinet shop with Swedes who spoke their native tongue, so lunch breaks must have been lonesome for him. Although Pop had been driving since he was a youngster, he could not pass the written driving test which of course was in English. So our new Chevrolet sat in the driveway for some time. The year we purchased our two-tone, green and crocus-yellow car, was also the first year that windshields were made of one piece of glass. This could have been the first and only time we purchased anything on a loan, because we were a cash-only family. Meanwhile Mom learned to drive, and soon the three of us were taking Sunday afternoon drives. This was not much fun since we usually got lost, and you know who had to ask directions and be the guide to get us back home.

Being Americans also meant television. Our first one was a Zenith with a 17" square screen, not the round one we watched at our neighbor's house in Holland. Some of our favorites were "I remember Mama," "Meet Milly," and the most memorable one, "The Hit Parade." Life was good even if I was not permitted to attend high school football games or any other sport events: sports were not considered part of education which is what school was for. I became infatuated with the theater. Two shows per year. I was either on stage or back stage! During my last two years of high school I created a real problem for my folks. I went steady with Danny, who was Jewish! We were happy dating each other even though our relationship was not received well at home.

I rushed into my American future without looking behind. Our life in Park Ridge, New Jersey, fell into a routine. Pop went back to cabinet making. Mom, who was an excellent cook, became a dietician in the schools. As a teenager, I eagerly embraced the excitement of learning a new language and the adventure of my new life. I now smiled for the camera. The émigré community in Midland Park quickly became yet another circle of villagers for me.

More Family

Once we were in New Jersey and settling into our life, we saw less of tante Ro and oom Nap van Gelder. I do not remember them coming to our home on Tuxedo Avenue although we were just a few miles apart. We did on occasion go to their house. When we visited, oom Nap showed his home movies, most usually of his California grandchildren, Jocelyn and Beverly. It was fun seeing the two girls running under the sprinkler, playing in the garden, and waving at the camera in the sunshine. Little did I know that oom Nap's grandchildren were my second cousins. I learned this in 2000, nearly fifty years later, when Jocelyn and Beverly finally came into my life. Tante Ro and oom Nap who became our sponsors in the United States never received credit for their help. Their sponsorship of Mom, Pop, and me remained unknown to me until 2000. It was not until then that I learned the full extent of my paternal family's involvement in our emigration process.

I do believe that Mom corresponded with Alice, how strange is that! The scheme of secrecy continued when aunt Alice and uncle Steven came to see Mom before they moved to Israel and asked to see me. They were invited to tea and they took a picture, which I later received in the mail. At the time, I was still confused, who were these visitors from California? The answer to my question was so vague that I knew not to probe. That photo made it easy for me to recognize Beverly in 2000 when I picked her up at the airport in Knoxville, because she strongly resembled her mother.

Tante Lena, a longtime friend of Mom and Pop, arrived several years later. She moved to America and visited with us in the early sixties. Tante Lena taught me how to sew on a sewing machine and to read and adjust a printed pattern. I was about to be married then and I purchased my own sewing machine. Mom's had always been off limits for me. It was old and operated by hand and no replacement parts were available. My first project was a gold-colored two-piece dress suit. I still had a lot to learn. Purchasing a lovely, dry-clean only wool cloth that needed to be lined was not a good first project. It was to be my Easter outfit, so I achieved the job. Pop, with his exacting carpenter eye always checked my hems. Even without measuring he could see if they were not absolutely straight.

Then oom Mark visited us briefly in Park Ridge with his second wife tante Joke. I do not recall this visit, but it is noted in my little green Poetry Book. The next time I heard from him was in the early 1960s. I was in my early twenties, and this was the first and only time that I communicated with a family member directly, without Mom. We corresponded about an inheritance and I gave him power of attorney. Mom and Pop were offended and objected to my dealing with him directly. Why, I was now an adult! Oom Mark's daughter was Jacqueline. She now lives in Israel with her daughter, a sweet and spunky lady with whom I still exchange an occasional email.

Tante Sien and oom Ies Spetter lived at 12 Everett Street in East Orange, New Jersey, after they were married on January 7, 1954. We became regular visitors to their home. I think we were invited to Thanksgiving dinners. They were just another aunt and uncle to me. The trips to their home are secured in my memory bank because we invariably got lost after exiting the Garden State parkway system. I was once more asking directions and then explaining them to whoever was driving, not fun! I very briefly dated oom Ies' grandson Nathan in the late fifties. Our relationship must have been acceptable to oom Ies' daughter Sara. By then I was in my mid-teens. Tante Sien and oom Ies remained very kind to us. After a while, we were driving their lovely black Buick with red leather interior and they were getting by with one car. It was another example of their generosity, probably a gift. It was not until 2000 that I learned how instrumental both must have been in our emigration process. Oom Ies and tante Sien ultimately decided to move back to The Netherlands. Oom Ies died in 1959 in Barendrecht. Tante Sien lived until 1975 and died in Driebergen, close to where her oldest son Jacques Landa lived.

I did not meet uncle Charles Reens until we arrived in the United States, even though he had been involved in my custody hearings. He was married to Esther van Creveld, a sister to the tantes. He must have traveled a lot, because Pop and I only visited him in his hotel rooms. There was a huge suitcase that fascinated me: it stood up on end like a portable closet. I was the princess of the day with my best dress, a light blue hand-me down from my cousin Jocelyn. It was made of stiff nylon embossed with white flocks of some birds. I think we visited him several times, just Pop and I together. Each time we came away with an envelope which I recognized to be American from its red and blue border. Hindsight tells me that this might have been a gift of money. This uncle Charles was much more casual than oom Carel Drukker, the piano teacher, they were almost opposites. I had no idea why we visited and of course did not know that we were related.

New Friends

As soon as Pop acquired his driver's license, our weekly trips to church began. I was to make my profession of faith. I was baptized in the spring of 1953 and joined the Christian Reformed church in Midland Park, New Jersey. I do not remember how we ended up going 40 minutes from our home in Park Ridge for church services at Bethel Christian Reformed Church on Haledon Avenue, in Prospect Park. I believe it was part of a grand plan. Initially someone, I do not remember who, brought us to church. One of the members became a close friend and our insurance agent. His name was oom Pete Damsma; his wife became another aunt to me. Except for them, we did not socialize. That is strange, because having a church family is a vital part of life. But we never loitered after services. Mom always led us out of the building very quickly, even though I was attending catechism classes and wanted to visit with my new friends. Confirmation classes met every week. They concluded in the spring, I remember that I wore a new outfit for the ceremony: a baby-blue striped suit with a straight

skirt and a three-quarter sleeves jacket. My white shoes had a wedge—
the first grown-up pair I owned. Several teens became members of the
church on that Sunday, but I was the only one baptized. The actual
ceremony is a vague memory, but I remember clearly that it was one
of those occasions where all this seemed to be happening to another
person. The feeling is difficult to explain. If I had been raised Jewish,
that would have been the time for my bat mitzvah.

Our weekly trips included Bible study at the Hymans home in
Patterson with a group of Dutch expatriates that included the Rever-
end Ernest Cassuto, the son of secular Jewish parents and a Holocaust
survivor. He lived with his family in Patterson. I visited their home and
played with their two twin daughters. After being imprisoned by the
Nazis and narrowly escaping death in 1944 thanks to a Dutch Christian underground worker, Cassuto converted to Roman Catholicism
and later became a minister in the Dutch Reformed Church. He eventually wrote his story *The Last Jew of Rotterdam* which was published in
1974. My life story intrigued him. Did he travel to the United States
on the same ship as we did? He too had emigrated in 1952 with his
wife Elizabeth. He asked Mom and Pop's permission to write my story.
They told him no. I was only a teenager and no one consulted me. That
ended our visits to his house. Not only did we not see him and Elly his
wife anymore, but I did not get to play with their twin babies.

CHAPTER 9

Becoming an American Citizen

I became an American citizen in 1959 while a senior at Park Ridge High School. I was eighteen years old and wise enough to make some of my own choices. Taking the citizenship test made me a true American citizen. That was simple enough, yet at this time another serious decision was made: I officially lost my birth name. The judge stamped on the back of the legal document that my name was now Sonja Elizabeth van der Kaden. How was all this manipulated behind my back?

As I understand it, up to that time I still owned my name Clara Van Thijn. I did not examine the back of the document until years later and then bemoaned the fact that I had no say in such a vital decision. Was this done to once again erase my past? If that was the intent, it certainly did not distance me from my dear birth parents. And anyways, soon thereafter I would become Sonja DuBois.

Our threesome family did not cut ties with Holland entirely. During the first summers, Mom went to visit her relations by herself and left me to care for Pop. Cooking things that were not our regular menu items were Pop's delight. I learned to prepare brains and other innards I choose to forget. Kidneys certainly fit into that category. I was too young to drive, and Pop was off to work during the day, so those months were boring.

When I was sixteen, the three of us went to Holland. The trip was not memorable except for Pamela the miniature pinscher dog. We stayed at oma Post's house and slept upstairs in the attic. Directly across the narrow street lived a young man who enjoyed making jokes about Pamela. I remember his last name as Verhoeven. As the designated dog walker, I suffered his jokes, "there goes the hamburger on a leash—*gehaktbal*." That was the start of our brief romance. We went to the movie theater where he worked. When the movie reel had to be turned, he dashed to the projection booth. That was the beginning of his career in film. I read not long ago that he became renowned in the film industry, probably in America. That summer, I was pressured to break off the relationship. My family said that I was being used because he needed to be sponsored to come to America. Another teenage crush that came and went. The only visit I made outside the immediate family was to the Poot family who had fed me during the war. They now lived in a modern apartment. I don't remember if we talked about the war. My activities were closely monitored anyway, because Mom did not want me to have any contact with the past. But I do recall tante Truus' husband oom Frans telling Mom and Pop that they were too strict with me.

CHAPTER 10

Ron

Meeting Ron

Soon after graduating from high school, I attended business college in New York City and commuted from Park Ridge every day. Often, large business offices had a proper maiden lady who was also a yenta and a matchmaker. That was the case at the Horrowitz Ravitch Horrowitz construction office where I was eventually hired. Even though Ron and I had met earlier and often spoken on the telephone, it was at the 1961 office Christmas party that Ms. White properly introduced us. We dated all the following summer. I think that on our first date we joined friends, picnicked, and swam in a lake in New Jersey. Our dates were mostly in New York City. I was so smitten with this older young man who escorted me to Broadway plays. It was really a fairy-tale romance. We dined at the Tavern on the Green and enjoyed some lovely weekend brunches there as well. The most memorable and fantastic dinner experience happened at the Piccadilly hotel. Its Swedish smorgasbord was such a magnificent spread. Fish and salads, meats and vegetables, and the beautifully displayed desserts and cheeses are never to be forgotten. Ron often wore a baby-blue seersucker suit which fit him perfectly. At that time, he smoked a pipe which added to the ambiance. We had common experiences in that he grew up in military schools and family life was absent.

Shortly after our engagement, commuting became less stressful. Initially Ron would bring me home to Park Ridge after a city date, then he would drive back home to Brooklyn. Late at night he would sometimes pull off the West Side Highway to catch a short nap. That was not dangerous in the sixties, and at times the police stopped and checked on him.

Even though Ron has lived in the South for many years, he still takes pride in the fact that he lived in all the Burroughs of New York except the Bronx. When we met, his bachelor apartment was in Brooklyn and he drove a 1958 white Chevrolet. It was his pride and joy. The tires make the memories. I will always remember how, one Christmas morning on West Side Highway, Ron calmly changed a flat tire with traffic zooming by in the next lane. His suit and fedora were never the same. When he lived in Brooklyn, he was a member of the 4th Presbyterian Church in Brooklyn. He has fond memories of his time there. We have always heard about his involvement in church life. Musicals were part of their ministry and his role as Curly in the Broadway play Oklahoma is a sweet memory.

Soon after we became engaged, Pop put his carpentry skills to work at home and what had been mere back steps became an enclosed porch, complete with a folding bed for my fiancé. Now Ron stayed until after Sunday church service and dinner. Ron especially enjoyed Mom's meals and ate just about anything. At one particular meal, we had rabbit, and Mom was sure that he would not recognize it. We did not tell him, thinking this would be a joke. When she asked if he liked the meat, he answered that he did enjoy the rabbit. It was a frequent fare when he was stationed in Germany during the Korean War. He had not been fooled after all!

When we asked for Mom and Pop's blessing, Ron wore what we knew in Holland as baker's pants, which Pop somehow thought was a good thing. The black-and-white checks helped smooth the way; their familiarity to Mom and Pop set the tone. Our wedding took place on May 12, 1962 at the Bethel Christian Reformed Church in Prospect Park. We had a guest or two from Beirut where Ron's dad has his roots. Together we are Jewish and Arabic, a combination that has worked for over fifty years. Ron and I have been together the better part of our lives. One of the reasons we are still best friends is that each of us often gives an extra measure of understanding and devotion. In Holland we have an expression which roughly translates as "every pot has a lid"—so it is with us. Our backgrounds are not really different. I did not have the warmth of a biological mother, and Ron lived in foster homes before attending military schools during his preteen and teenage years. Looking back, we learned a lot from each other when we became a family. Our love and devotion to each other have grown during the many years of our marriage, and thanks to my dear husband, we now even finish each other's sentences. I look back and think how often we took life for granted! Ron is a gentle soul and has a quiet temperament, somewhat different from mine, and that is an understatement!

I lived at home until I became Mrs. DuBois. Ron and I married in the same church where I made my profession of faith. After our marriage, we continued to call Bethel our home church until Monique, our first-born baby, was a few months old. By then, traveling a long distance each week became cumbersome, so we joined the Presbyterian Church in Westwood which was a mere 15-minute drive from our home. That seems like a peculiar method to choose a church, but we were happy there. We moved to Florida in 1977 so that Ron could earn a Master's degree in building construction management. His education had begun in 1958 at Fairleigh Dickinson University and continued on and off until his graduation in 1978 from the University of Florida. This again demonstrates his quiet persistence. It took the support of our entire family. The girls were in their pre-teens when we lived in Florida for one year, and they often remind us of the sacrifice they made for the family venture by having to share a bedroom. Looking back, they did enjoy the experience. Fortunately, riding their bikes to school on the sidewalk and swimming in the apartment complex pool balanced things. After Ron's graduation, we moved to Knoxville and have lived in the same house since arriving in 1979.

A Recipe for Jan Hagel Cookies

There were two basic kinds of cookies when I was growing up. One was served to guests and the other was for kids. The *Jan Hagel* definitely was a cookie served to guests who came for tea. For a youngster in my day, it was like a rite of passage to be served a treat out of the fancy tin kept for the purpose of sharing the best current recipe of the house. Now let me tell you how a recipe of this high caliber became known as "Daddy cookies" in our family.

As a bride, I received an unusual gift from my new husband. One evening he brought me a package. It was a measuring scale with grams clearly marked on its dial face. It took me just a little while to understand the meaning of this shiny and unusual gift. My Ron's favorite recipes were from the old country, the country of my birth. He quickly learned that the cup and ounce measurements did not apply, so he bought this new gadget. He certainly knew how to ensure the continuation of his favorite treats. The scale still has a place high on top of the kitchen cabinets as a bit of nostalgia. It has not been in service for many years. All of our old favorites have been simplified and transposed to standard American cups.

Before we set out the recipe's ingredients, I need for you to know that modern products have minimized the job of baking these rich, buttery, sweet treats, while causing some changes to the original recipe. The best time saver has been shaved and peeled almonds. The old-time way is to bring some almonds in their brown shells to a quick boil and cool to a temperature where they can be peeled and chopped. Another change is in the sugar topping sprinkled on top of the cookies just before they are popped into the oven. In all my searching, I have never found the very small chunks of crystal sugar we used to sprinkle and pat down on the dough. Anyhow try these, for grownups only of course.

¾ cup butter (don't compromise by using margarine)
1¾ cup flour (I always use unbleached in all my baking, more nutrients)
½ cup sugar
a pinch of salt

Mix ingredients together and press into a small jelly-roll pan.

Mix **1 egg** with a few drops of water, use half of the mixture and spread on dough.

Sprinkle with **pearl sugar** about 3 tbsp. and **slivered almonds**, press in gently.

Heat the oven to 350°F and bake for 20 minutes. Cut into 3" squares while still warm in the pan. Enjoy!

PART FOUR

OLD VILLAGERS RETURN

CHAPTER 11

Renewing Friendships

When I was raising my family, Schifrah did not exist. I barely remember the attempts I made to research my history because they did not reveal anything and I became thoroughly discouraged. The past, however, refused to be totally buried. When Ron and I moved into our first home, Pop brought a picture to me. He had made a light oak frame for it and he told me "Keep this, because it belongs to your family." It was only after 2001 that I fully understood what he meant.

In 1965, when baby Monique was about 7 months old, my Jewish and foster relatives thought Ron should get to know family members. And so we traveled to Holland. We were hosted by Jacques Detiger' parents in Schiedam. Tante Truus lived around the block from where we used to live and often took care of Monique. The language barrier did not exist between them and they were both content. That made it easier for us to travel and see Mom's friends, nieces and nephews. The only visit we all made together was to tante Sien. We also had tea with her daughter Josephiena whom I used to see at tante Sien when I was growing up in Schiedam. I did not see anyone else from my birth family.

In 1976 we returned to Holland, but this trip left many gaps in my memory. I do remember visiting Toepad, the Jewish cemetery in Rotterdam. It was eerie! When we were gathered on the grounds and the car was empty, its horn sounded repeatedly. We were searching for my grandfather Benjamin de Vries' grave, which was unmarked. We eventually found it because of the precise Dutch card system. Ron took a picture of me by his grave. Benjamin de Vries was killed in 1943 by the Nazi occupation forces while recuperating in a hospital. I also noticed the Drukkers' graves, in particular that of Rozalie van Straaten and others too whom I now know to be relatives. Hans, a friend of the Drukker or Creveld family, asked around for some additional information about the gravesites. We exchanged some emails for several years. He died in 1999. Recently, I learned that tante Dien, the Drukkers' only daughter, wrote their family story. That is how long one sometimes has to wait for the full story to be told.

CHAPTER 12

Meeting Dolf

After we emigrated to the United States, Willy, my grade school friend, and I stayed in touch. We wrote each other, and I visited her when I went with Mom and Pop to the Netherlands for our summer vacation. By the mid-1980s, the United States Holocaust Memorial Museum was being planned, and, with the easing of Cold War tensions and the opening up of Eastern European countries, an increasing number of survivors tried finding out more about their past and reconnected with other survivors. This is when my story was "rediscovered" thanks to Dolf Henkes. Willy helped reconstruct my journey from the time of my rescue by Dolf Henkes. She was instrumental in reuniting me with him forty-five years later.

For many years, Dolf remained *persona non grata*. I had only heard he lived in a bad part of town, was a Catholic, a homosexual, and an artist, different from anyone I had ever associated with. Of course, I believed what Mom and Pop said about him. Knowing him and acknowledging his part in my survival would take away from what Mom and Pop did for me.

On November 22, 1985, Dolf posted a short ad in *Het Nieuw Israëlietisch Weekblad*, requesting anyone who knew what had happened to me to contact him. The Rotterdam (weekly) newspaper *Het Nieuwe Stadsblad* published an interview with Dolf on Wednesday December 4, 1985, along with my school picture. Written by Ruud van Houwelingen, *Het Nieuwe Stadsblad* article was entitled "Joods drama herleeft in Schiedam: Waar is Claartje toch gebleven?" [Jewish drama is relived in Schiedam: What Has Become of Claartje?]. It read:

> *Schiedam—The well-known painter and Rotterdam visual artist Dolf Henkes (82), who had several exhibitions at the Schiedam Municipal Museum, sits at the end of the day with a very pressing question: What has become of Claartje? The story goes back to the dark days of 1940-1945, especially the darkest chapter of this period, the deportation of many Jewish Netherlanders. Two of them were the van Thijn-de Vries couple from Rotterdam. Before and during the first years of World War II, he was the director of a trading company of meat byproducts in Rotterdam. The couple had one daughter Claartje, who was born just before the war and thus must now be 45 or 46 years old.*
>
> *From Het Steiger in Rotterdam where the van Thijns and Claartje first lived, they had to move to Vierambachtstraat in Rotterdam. That was out of necessity because Het Steiger was bombed during May 1940 and completely destroyed.*
>
> *At Vierambachtstraat, the drama began for the van Thijn couple. The first transport of Jews began in 1942 and the van Thijns reported for the fourth transport.*
>
> ### Downfall
>
> *Dolf Henkes, now 82 years old, sees it as a film more than 43 years ago. "I was close friends with the van Thijns," he says. "I asked and begged them not to go because this would be their downfall. I had proof that the Nazis were planning to transport the Dutch Jews and kill them, but no matter how much I talked, it had no effect. Van Thijn said, "I belong to my group and will not shirk my responsibility." But they wanted to give up their only daughter Claartje (now 45 or 46 years old).*
>
> *The van Thijns went by way of Rotterdam, Westerbork in Drenthe, to Germany, most likely the death camp of Bergen Belsen and nobody ever heard from them again.*

Then the drama continued, initially with the afore-named Claartje van Thijn and Dolf Henkes in the lead roles. "There was a hiding place for the van Thijns in the Achterhoek. But these people did not want to take her, so I took the daughter in as a foundling and in 1942 she was placed with a foster family in Schiedam."

Van der Kaden

Dolf Henkes: "The only thing that I can now remember is that the foster family, named van der Kaden, had no children and lived near the center of Schiedam. They lived in a big house, the foster father was a carpenter, and the house had a big brown door.

Since that time Dolf Henkes never had any contact with Claartje. He does know that the foster father van der Kaden took a job with the Holland America Line, and around 1948 he left for the United States with his wife and Claartje. That is where the trail ends. The van der Kadens became very attached to their foster child and did not want to have any contact with her rescuer. All other attempts to contact Claartje van der Kaden, as her maiden name undoubtedly now reads, have failed.

Family

She must have (distant) relatives living in Schiedam and perhaps acquaintances from the last years of World War II and the postwar years, before the Van der Kadens emigrated to the United States.

"Somebody must know something about her," says Dolf Henkes, now living in his home at the Veerlaan in Katendrecht. "I would appreciate it so much if I could be in touch with Claartje one more time."

If anyone knows her address, he/she can contact Mr. Dolf Henkes at 010-852428. The people of Schiedam who knew Claartje and know her present whereabouts would fulfill a life wish of the 82-year old artist from Rotterdam, Dolf Henkes.

Het Nieuwe Stadsblad published a follow-up article a few days after its initial query, reporting about the developments. The article was entitled: "Joods meisje opgespoord. Claartje is nu Sonja" [Jewish girl found. Claartje is now Sonja].

Schiedam. The call of the 82-year old painter Dolf Henkes: "What has become of Claartje?" has not remained unanswered. Het Nieuwe Stadsblad had barely rolled off the presses when the telephone started ringing at Dolf Henkes' home on the Veerlaan in Rotterdam.

"I have not been away from the phone in three days," he says. "I did not count the number of phone calls, but it must be in the hundreds."

The burning question of course was: "What has become of Claartje?"

In any case, it is clear that Claartje was renamed Sonja by her foster parents, that she is happily married, has two children, and lives in the United States.

"Things are particularly good for her," say many Schiedammers who still are in touch with her. Will Dolf Henkes try to make contact with Sonja now? "No," he says, "I think that would be indiscreet. I wanted to know in the final days of my life if she is still living and if she is happy. "These two questions have been answered and that makes me especially happy," continues Mr. Henkes. "I don't know if she wants to be confronted with the tragic past of her parents who were both killed in 1942 in Bergen Belsen."

Does Sonja or Claartje know who her real parents were? Says Dolf Henkes: "It might open painful wounds. I am happy that everything ended well and that she is happy. Perhaps she will be given this news via her Schiedam acquaintances and she will make contact with me. I will not seek contact with her, because maybe she would not appreciate it."

Mom and Pop received copies of the newspaper articles but did not forward them to me. Cousins on Mom's side also read the articles but were told not to forward them to me. They did not think highly of Dolf, because the chicken coop story at Schapedoorn had been distorted. They distrusted his motives for granting the interview. They believed that he had cared for me for his own benefit and now wanted some reward for his action. It was Willy who sent the articles to me. I was surprised by the first article, but not by the photo. My picture had been taken at school when I was a toddler, and I remember a teacher handing a picture over the fence to someone. Today I am pretty sure that it was Dolf Henkes to whom my teacher handed the picture he used in the 1985 article. This brought back the feelings I had when I was talked about—knowing without knowing that my parents never returned, from where and why they never returned, piecing my story together over several years, and feeling somehow different. Back then, people must have thought that little kids don't have ears.

Willy soon learned about the articles from her sister and knew right away that Claartje and I were the same person. She later wrote:

It was indeed Sonja. There was a phone number. I called first thing in the morning to learn what this gentleman wanted with Sonja. He turned out to be just a nice man who wanted to know if Sonja lived, and if she was happy. Dolf Henkes said that he had been a friend of Sonja's father and that he knew her when she was very little. He also had a few things of hers that he had kept and wanted to give to her. Could I reassure him about her fate?

Not knowing if Sonja was informed about her origins by her foster parents, I decided to gently ask her. In my best English (which then was not bad) I wrote a letter to Sonja. It was one of the hardest letters I have written. Sonja called me back asking how I came in contact with this man. I explained the circumstances to her. Dolf and I made an appointment for me to come and collect her things. Dolf turned out to be an old, simple, and very friendly man. He was emotional when I came inside his apartment. His sister Marie was there, a very sweet woman. Dolf asked me what I knew about Sonja. I did not want to trouble them, so I just told him a few things and showed him Sonja's wedding picture. This made him very happy. We struck up a conversation and I told him the story I had heard about Sonja being a foundling. Dolf said that it was not true. He talked about his friendship with Sonja's father and mother.

They had bought one of his first paintings. The agreement was that Dolf would make another large painting for them. For inspiration, with a theme from before the war. Early on, when there were raids on Jewish people, Sonja's father was fired because the Germans wanted him to become desperate and to see that someday they would be picked up. Her parents hoped to be able to save their lives by complying, and to survive the camps. To my surprise, Dolf said that in 1942 he already knew of the extermination camps. He stated that he knew because he was in the resistance. (It was only in 1944 that the public learned that they were not labor camps). Sonja's parents were afraid to get off the train (there were heavily armed soldiers near the train ready to shoot those who fled). In the end Dolf was able to convince the parents to entrust Sonja to him. [...] It was an emotional moment, and Dolf was crying. I understood that he must have loved his friend very much.

Marie, Dolf's sister, agreed that Sonja's parents were such lovely people, and that they (Dolf, Marie and an unnamed brother) missed them all. Dolf said he had gone with Sonja to Overijssel. There lived a friend whom he trusted. He himself could not keep Sonja because the Germans searched each property for Jews. It was too dangerous because children were taken. In the province there was much less control. The friend wanted no part in taking hiding persons, no child. After much talking, Sonja was finally taken to the henhouse for the night. Dolf was shocked that a friend would do such a thing! When telling me the story, Dolf and Marie were weeping. Dolf painted this trip. A farmhouse with the brown cloud. (The brown was for the SS uniform). Dolf tried for a couple of days more to find something for Sonja in Overijssel. He had no luck. Dolf took Sonja back to Rotterdam. It became increasingly dangerous, because Dolf was in the resistance. Therefore, he put out a (Resistance) newspaper advertisement. In a kind of code. The van der Kadens responded.

Because the foster parents wanted no further contact after the war, Dolf hadn't seen or heard from her ever since. It was a sad emotional visit. At the end of the evening Marie gave to me a necklace and spoon with the request to give them to Sonja. More they had not.

Since 1987 was the year of our 25th wedding anniversary, Ron and I celebrated the occasion by going to Holland, thereby fulfilling Mr. Henkes' wish to see Clara once more. But I was reluctant to visit Dolf. Mom and Pop knew that I was going. Pop had told me, I know what you are doing; when you go, you will have more questions than answers. He urged me not to open Pandora's box. That visit was my first step in transgressing Mom and Pop's rules. I acknowledged to myself that Dolf had played an important part in my rescue and was the first and most important link in my network of villagers who were risking their lives to save Jewish children during the war. I still did not feel that I could accept or reciprocate Dolf's caring for me. During the visit, I felt like I was cheating on Mom and Pop.

Willy provided support and accompanied me to visit Dolf and his sister Marie. I was daunted by the past because my curiosity had been discouraged, even forbidden for so many years. Therefore, when Dolf and I met, I did not ask the questions that I burned to have answers to.

I have often wondered and still wonder in what circumstances Dolf and my Daddy met. To the best of my knowledge at the time, Dolf was the first person I met who knew daddy personally. There was so much more to be revealed. Dolf also wanted to give me what I now realize was the Schapedoorn painting, but I refused. Here is how Willy tells the story of that visit:

A couple of months later, Sonja came to the Netherlands and was staying with me. I called Dolf whether he wanted to see Sonja. He really wanted to, but Sonja did not really want to. I had not foreseen that! I felt that Dolf deserved the visit. Sonja was cool while visiting Dolf. I felt terrible. He and his sister did not deserve this. He took us to his studio. There Sonja could have figured things out. She did not. Dolf saw that I had a lot of grief from her attitude. He motioned for me to let it go.

Apparently, Dolf was very moved by the visit. Willy writes:

> *Later, I went back to Dolf and Marie. They were physically weaker. Dolf told me, I'm so happy to have seen her. It is not about whether they found us to be nice. I found out that I did not get her out of that train for nothing. That was my last visit to Dolf. At Christmas, I sent a card. I got a copy of one of his paintings as a Christmas card. That was the last I heard from them. Shortly after they died.*

After that visit, I went to Westerbork, the camp where Dutch Jews were held before their final ride to Auschwitz. I discovered the specific deportation train which carried my parents to their death in August 1942. My past continued to be shrouded in silence. Neither the few surviving birth relatives nor my foster family ever broke the silence. They passed on before I learned the whole story.

PART FIVE

FROM DOUBT TO ACCEPTANCE

CHAPTER 13

Family Finds Me

Cousin Beverly

My renewed search for the past began with a telephone call in November 1998: "I think we are cousins." The voice was my cousin Beverly's. Her family was fortunate. Before she was born, three family members escaped on the last ship to leave Rotterdam before the German Invasion. They left on May 1, 1940. Our grandmothers were sisters. At last the silence was broken. The yarn unraveled after that first telephone message. The internet proved a fantastic help in discovering who I am.

In 2000, I traveled to Israel where they now live, to meet Beverly, her sister Jocelyn, and their mother, aunt Alice. I had always hoped to speak to someone who knew my parents. That wish came true when I met aunt Alice, and I made wonderful discoveries about other distant relations. Thanks to Beverly's extensive genealogical research, I know something of my paternal grandmother's family. Aunt Alice and daddy were cousins and good friends when they were teens. They went on bicycle excursions together. I also met members of our family who live in Israel. There is where I met Jacqueline. I always called her Rootje. It was there that I saw for the first time a picture of my parents culled from a short reel of Alice's wedding before the war. I was 60 when this actually became the photo I treasure. It was then that I knew that I looked like my mother. My parents on that photo were twenty-four years old.

Sadly, people who could today provide more information have died or are nearing the end of their life. I may never know more of my history or learn more about my family, because too much time has elapsed. There have been many disappointments even from my late discoveries. I am sorry that I never knew Beverly and Jocelyn's parents as aunt Alice and uncle Steven. Like the few distant birth relatives who survived the war, they stayed in the shadows of my life. It appears that they were a major influence in my life. I will always feel indebted to them.

What is important is that, although I was still a floating puzzle piece, I began finding places where I fit. I started reading non-fiction books in the Judaic section of the bookstore and library, and slowly acquired a small Judaic library myself. More importantly, the need to connect with my biological family increased as a result.

Writing My Mother's Story

Writing in earnest about my lost childhood began before 1998. I needed to be a part of my biological mother Sophie's life during the dreadful times of the early 1940s, from the time when Jews had to report to the Nazi occupying authorities until a few days before giving me up. I wrote letters in my mother's voice. I needed to feel close to her by imagining her life during these stressful months. Even though this may seem strange, I now understand that this is not an unusual method of coping. For a time, I became Sophie. I imagined a young mother's loneliness and anxiety. I corresponded with her cousin Alice who escaped the horror of the Holocaust in the nick of time, and who understood the war-time conditions in Holland. I attempted to bond with the mother I do not remember. With these letters and diary pages, I learned to process my losses and say goodbye.

Rotterdam, 5 November 1940
Dear Alice,
We have not written in so long that I do not know where to begin. We were bombed out of our house in May of this year. Fortunately, Mau was home. The end of the building got a direct hit, and ours

shook before it started to burn. It was the beginning of a relentless assault. Our beautiful historic downtown is one big pile of rubble. Planes are often heard whistling by at night, but this attack came in the afternoon. As you know, we always have suitcases packed in case we have to flee or hide from German troops. We grabbed some of our photo albums and wedding gifts and Mau took a few of his precious canvases and his paint box. We ran to Mau's dad, Abe's store. It all happened so fast that it took me days to realize what could have become of us.

We stayed with Mau's parents, Abe and Sarah, in the Oranjeboomstraat for a while. It is close to Katendrecht, away from the city center. As their apartment above the store is not suited for extra people, we started looking for our own place within a couple of days. I am happy to let you know that we found such a place and now live just a street away from our friends, Sara and Schmuel, on Vierambachtstraat in the western part of town. So that softens the blow somewhat. Not only do we see them often, but the fact that we suffer the same predicament makes all this a bit more tolerable.

Sara has been great in helping us to settle in the new neighborhood. She even took me to the greengrocer and introduced us to Tony. He helps some of the young Jewish mothers. He does what he can, sometimes smuggling extra potatoes or fruit into our baskets. That makes me think of you. Whenever I use our basket, I remember when we bought it at the mart, do you? We met at Sara's for coffee, and then you two pushed your babies in their carriages while I waddled along and we shopped at our usual mart.

You too are in transit! From Curaçao to New York City: what a risky time for such perilous travel. But at least in New York, you will easily find your parents. They should be a great help to you. I know you are probably not at your new home yet, but thought it would be nice for you to have a greeting when you arrive. It's clever to have a "postbus" while you are without a permanent address. Will you get an apartment right away or will you stay in a hotel until you get

*settled? I hope you did not get seasick on your way across the ocean.
It would be hard to take care of the baby if you were not feeling well.
Aren't you glad she is not crawling yet? I know we were eager for that
to happen before you left Rotterdam but it is lots easier not to have
to chase her around. The surroundings can't be very clean on a boat
with so many passengers aboard. Have you met anyone you know?
Didn't Steven have some acquaintances from Germany who were
trying to get passage as well? Anyhow we think of you every day and
pray for your safety.*

*I so wish that you could see our baby Clara who was born almost
a month ago today. She is such a tiny creature and not nursing very
well either. Naturally that makes me anxious, for we were just rationed on meat and butter. I can't afford to become undernourished
while I am trying to feed her. It's a shame that the very products that
are the staples of our country are becoming scarce. It's probably the
export, don't you think?*

*You and Steven were so brave to take your new baby to an un-
known place. I wish we had the courage to escape. That is no longer
possible. Our friend Dolf tells us that it is very difficult to get a departure visa for Belgium and France.*

*It is time to get ready for the aunties, they are coming to tea so
they can see their little niece. I'll visit with you again soon and finish
this letter so it can be mailed.*

Love from us,
Mau, Sophie & Clara

....

Rotterdam, 25 December 1940
Dear Alice,
*I was so happy to receive your letter, and to hear that all of you are
settled in an apartment of your own. Have you found a baby carriage
yet? Soon Jocy will be ready for a stroller though. Is the food much
different from what you are used to in Holland? I imagine America
has some different foods. Are there many fruits and vegetables?*

Here food is becoming very scarce; the troops eat first. We are rationed of course and need stamps for almost everything we can purchase. The problem is that the stamps only allow you to buy so much. Our main concern is for the baby. Clara is not growing as much as her doctor says she needs to. My milk is just not nurturing her, so our pediatrician did give me some extra food stamps and I will have to give her a bottle a few times a day. There is a special powder that one mixes with boiled water to produce formula which is supposed to taste much like my own milk. We just started the procedure last evening and Clara does not seem to mind the change.

I am beginning to wonder if it was wise for us to stay here now that we are really controlled by Hitler's Nazi forces. It is too late now to obtain a visa; one of Mau's coworkers was just denied. It's so sad since they had a sponsor and a home ready for them in Canada.

Mau's company has been closed. The offices were destroyed during the bombing and many people had to be laid off from work. Mau is still tracking shipments and financial transactions for the company, but I am afraid that this will soon be over and that he will have to find something else to do.

Love from us,
Mau, Sophie & Clara

....

Rotterdam, 13 February 1941
Dear Alice,
I just wanted to visit with you while Clara and Mau are in the backyard. That is the only improvement at our new address, the tiny brick patio with room to plant some flowers near the wooden fence. Two awful things happened to us since you received a letter. The reason Mau is home in the middle of the day is that he is out of his old job and may not have a new one . . . Then there is the compulsory registration of Jews that was issued last month . . .

I think Mau is going to register at the post office this week. It is required of all Jews and he says we should, since we take pride in our heritage. Being stopped on the street without proof of registration can be fatal. We have heard that Jews have been beaten by German sympathizers. We are no longer welcome in the cinema and students are barred from university. To identify us from everyone else, we may soon have to wear the yellow Star of David, as we hear is happening abroad. We would not be ashamed to wear it, although this would prevent us even more from doing the things we have been used to all our lives.

Who ever thought that Holland would crumble under Nazi rule? Your Steven did, and that is why you and your family escaped just in time!

Love, Sophie

· ·

Rotterdam, 8 April 1941

Dear Alice,

My answer to your letter is a few weeks late. Since you wrote, some of the answers to your questions have changed. During the last week of January, Mau's job was eliminated. He received a very complimentary letter to be used in seeking new employment. The shipments are still missing and there is simply no money left.

As far as seeking new employment, that's such a joke! As of last month, Jews no longer can own a business and others are threatened, to say the least, when they hire one of us. So now Mau is home all the time, he goes to visit with his friends. You may not know this, but the latest Nazi rules gave us another curfew. We are just furious, but quite helpless. We are forbidden to go to restaurants or cafés where the rest of the Dutch folks go. All signs are the same: 'Joden Verboden.' That does not leave us much freedom. So now Mau and his father visit in the back of Henri's tobacco shop. That's a good thing. At least he has not given up his beloved pipe. He must be anticipating that sacrifice as well, since he does not light up as often.

We are so happy to have your carriage, our wheels give us a chance to take Clara out. She now sits up with pillows propping her, which gives her a chance to see out and provides a nice change of scenery. Mau does not want us to wander too far, and of course he can't go with us. There have been several roundups this year. He is scared we might become mixed up in the chaos. Mostly we go to the aunties. They still have enough food to share and don't seem to be curtailed by the ration cards. Since there are three of them, they seem to be able to get along better than most of us. So, we are always welcome and often go right after Clara's nap. She only takes one now, so we get there early afternoon for tea. Usually there is pound cake. Sometimes instead of tea they have simmered a pot of soup, you remember the fragrance of their Shabbat chicken soup, don't you? We start back before four o'clock and get home so Clara can play with her daddy while I prepare dinner.

Speaking of Shabbat, we are hoping the grandparents will be able to visit on Friday. They'll be here by mid-afternoon and they'll stay until Saturday morning. I have hoarded two measures of white flour. So I will surprise everyone when the candles are lit; we will enjoy a lovely challah. I need to end, dear Alice, and run this to the post office. Write soon, love to Steven and your lovely little Jocy.
Love, Sophie

....

New York, 13 May 1941
Dear Sophie,
I hope you received the package we sent in March. I took it to the post office, at the same time that I collected your letters. I too have much to tell you and do not know quite where to begin. We are adjusting nicely to our new life, we live near my parents who asked oom Ies to book our passage from Curaçao to New York. I noticed that it took just four weeks for your last letter to reach us. Also, Steven received a letter from a former colleague in Germany which had been opened!

Are you aware that mail is being censored? Why on earth is that happening? We have heard from others that much of life in Europe is now being controlled because of the war.

I hope you have made friends in your new neighborhood. Fortunately you still have Sara and Schmuel. In a few months her Aaron and your little Clara will likely become playmates. We are so very thankful that you and the family were not harmed during the bombing. We have seen pictures of the terrible damage to Rotterdam during the German attack. Everyone knows why the Nazis bombed the city almost immediately, to force Dutch surrender. Rubble and more rubble, we could not find any of the familiar landmarks. The newsreels showed more than we wanted to see.

So where have you put the crib Sara gave you? Since you now have only one bedroom, you must be squeezed. What pieces of your new furniture were you able to rescue? Sara wrote me and said that you and Mau actually went back to the smoking rubble to recover some of your precious possessions. I am so sorry that you were not able to find the menorah. It has been in the family for a very long time. Steve's mother remembers grandmother polishing the slender silver columns when it was brought out of the china closet before Hanukah. Of course you are not to blame, Mau as the oldest son has a right to grandma's heirlooms.

Jocy will not need her jacket and knitted dresses for a while, so, we made a package for both of you. I know you can always use an extra blanket. Even during the rainy season doesn't get cold enough to wear our Dutch woolies. There are some wonderful yarn shops in town, so I am sending some wool along. Your talent will likely make them into a pretty dress for your precious little one. Send me a picture if you can, although never mind, let's not take a chance and alert anyone about the Jewish baby.

Write again soon but be cautious about everything!!

Love, Alice

••••••••••••••••••••••••••••••••••

Rotterdam, 18 June 1941

Dear Alice,

At home, Mau is often morose. He is worried about many things, in particular Jewish firms being closed down. The Nazi rules are making it difficult to live a normal life. Jews are often harassed on the bus so now my dear Mau gets up while it is still dark and walks for nearly an hour to the office. Fortunately, he found a job in the family business with van Creveld and Frenk. His expertise in the meat business is serving him well.

Several weeks ago, we heard a huge explosion. Allied planes had bombed the shipyards west of the city. Not knowing what to expect next, Mau decided that we should go to Sara's cove. That is what we call the hideout. There, we found Schmuel, Aaron and Sara who had the same idea. Schmuel and Mau had spent weeks preparing the emergency shelter. It was the friendliest place imaginable. Schmuel had whitewashed the walls and built a storage unit. Mau then painted nature scenes on the walls reminiscent of the parks we visited on our bike rides. All of us brought some household items. On the highest shelf of the shelter there is a mini-medicine chest with aspirin and children' cough medicine. The other bare necessities were mattress pads, a pump, and blankets. There was not enough room for a crib, but there was a small mattress for Aaron. Clara slept in her bassinet. Our aunties saved some of their food coupons for us and we were able to assemble a small larder with cans of stew, dry milk and baby cereal.

Our very dear friends made us welcome and we shared their food and rooms. Only the children were able to sleep. Since the Nazi soldiers were enforcing an all-day curfew, we had to stay together in our somewhat cozy prison. Schmuel defied both orders to relinquish his radio, so we eventually heard about the extent of the raid and found out that it was safe to return next morning.

Love, Sophie

....

Rotterdam, 18 June 1941
Dear Alice,
We receive mail three times a week now. That is quite a change from our usual twice a day delivery. It was wonderful to receive that yellow postal note which tells us to come and get a package. I couldn't wait for Mau to take care of it. You know that he does not like for us to walk to the post office by ourselves, but I took a chance and bundled Clara in her carriage so I could retrieve the package before he came home.

Since the girls have the same coloring and dark eyes, you know the dress is just perfect. Clara will be able to wear it this fall. The blanket and goodies are also appreciated. Thank you very much! You must know how we miss all of you, our dear cousins. I am glad we can still write to each other.

We are glad we decided to stay in our apartment. The bedroom is snug with the crib in it. It is comforting to have the three of us together, especially at dawn. That is when the planes whistle through the air. We never know if it is a flyover or if another attack is coming.

Going to the mart on Thursdays is hardly worth the trouble nowadays. The only cheese still available is young and flavorless. Not much fruit arrives at the stands. It is waylaid and eaten by the soldiers. The only thing worthwhile was the herring stand. Fish is so difficult to get so the smell of fresh fish makes my mouth water. Whenever he can, Mau brings some on his way home from his visit to Schmuel's studio. As a matter of fact, Sara and little Aaron were still here last week when he came home, so we all ate together. Too bad the little ones are too small to eat nutritious grownup fare, especially our frail Clara. I don't think I told you that our pediatrician referred us to a new office. He is no longer allowed to have Jewish patients. His office was very sorry and sent us a letter suggesting another office. It is the same one Sara uses, Dr. Goudsmit. The staff at the pediatrician's office must really feel bad about dismissing us. They sent several extra milk coupons along with the letter. That is so necessary, for Clara is really tiny. I guess there is nothing else they could do, since the authorities check their records to see if they serve any Jewish patients.

Last Sunday afternoon we went to the park with Sara and Schmuel as we have done since the tulips flowered. We walked along the Kralingse Plas and watched some folks sail and row. Rowboats are no longer rented to us, but we were glad to enjoy the sunshine together. We spread a blanket on the grass. Aaron is becoming steadier on his little feet and ended up walking behind his stroller. Clara is still content to be strolled around, although she is beginning to walk. We had no lunch but we had biscuits for the little ones to nibble.

The cookies you sent will be a perfect treat for our weekly picnics in the park. Fortunately the aunties came for tea yesterday and brought some homemade bread. I was able to tuck a few slices away, so I can make a few sandwiches with cheese from the mart. We are really excited, since we have not been able to have any family fun lately.

Please stay in touch. I will let you know what I make with the lovely yarn you sent. I am still hunting for just the right pattern!

Love to all of you,

Sophie

....

Rotterdam, 7 January 1942

Dear Alice,

Our dear friend Schmuel is missing! We are so very upset. As much as she will allow it we have been nurturing his wife Sara and little Aaron, who is thankfully too young to feel the full impact of this horror. All we know is that Schmuel was delivering one of his paintings to a prospective client when he was waylaid. When he did not return before curfew, Sara came to see us. She was frantic with worry. Of course we did not want her to go back to her apartment that late, but she could not be persuaded to stay with us. She wanted to be there in case someone would bring a message. She did allow us to keep baby

Aaron overnight. I made him a little bed in the Morris chair, and brought him back to her on Wednesday morning.

We are helpless in trying to find out where they have taken our friend. It happened on Tuesday afternoon and it is now Friday morning, of course we are worried sick. We think he was taken to Westerbork, the camp for Dutch Jews near the German border. Yesterday we sent a message to Mr. Cohen, his former employer, and hope that he can find the answer. He still has connections in places that we do not.

Our treats from the aunties are very rare now that they have left their home. The Nazis set up an office on their first floor, and they were afraid to stay in the same house. So a dear friend offered to take all three of them in his attic. We do not know who or where of course, but trust that they are safe. I hope the aunties stashed their paintings in a safe place. We hear that art works from many vacated homes are shipped to Germany, like many other goods. Likely they are gone forever! We hope that Mau is continuing to paint, especially now that his best friend and art comrade is missing.

The only good thing I want to tell you about is that I have started to knit Clara a new dress. It gives me a lot of pleasure to forget while I knit the pretty yarn you sent.

Best to you Steven, Jocy, and your Mom and Dad.

Love, Sophie

....

New York City, 15 February 1942
Dear Sophie,
I hope your ears have been ringing, we have been speaking about you, Schmuel and Sara. I just came back from the post office and received your letter telling us about Schmuel's disappearance. Steven and he were classmates and have been friends for at least a decade. We realize that Sara must be crazy with worry. I know your family will embrace her during these dark days. You must never give up hope! We had a letter, heavily censored, from one of Steven's colleagues last

week. We learned that his parents and young sister disappeared but showed up at their door in the middle of the night a week later. No one is talking about that lost week.

There is a package on the way with coffee and peanut butter, which I know is a favorite. The spring yarns are here, so there is a little special surprise in there for you. We cannot send tobacco products and do not want to take a chance that your package might be confiscated. But Steven often talks about the relaxation he enjoys when he lights up his pipe; that makes him think of Mau who must be low on tobacco.

I hope that Mau is in a frame of mind to continue his art. Painting is a great diversion, and at least he probably still has plenty of supplies. Our dad was just beginning to try his hand at oils and purchased materials to last a long time. Since he left everything behind, his hobby was cut short; we are glad that Mau can use the materials.

Jocy is beginning to talk more, mostly groups of words, not yet sentences. These are often a combination of Dutch and English. We are eager for her to retain her original language and we speak Dutch at home and with my parents. More and more, Jocy answers us in English. That will give her a good start when she starts school either here or in California, where I hope we will eventually settle. We all consider New York City a temporary homestead. I look forward to having the three of you close by after the war. Perhaps we will be on the same street. The girls can visit and build the same special relationship we have enjoyed for so long.

Love to you, Alice

••••••••••••••••••••••••••••••••••••

New York City, 31 March 1942
Dear Sophie,
You are probably correct in assuming that they took Schmuel to Westerbork, which as you know has been a refugee camp for foreign Jews for a few years. Steven has two friends who were just imprisoned there. If that is the case, Sara may hear from Schmuel soon. Inmates

are allowed one initial letter home. Although the mail is censored, at least, Sara will know where he is. Another of Steven's friends, Abe, says that life is not too awful there and that there is enough to eat. Abe's girlfriend, who was captured at the same time, was allowed to bring her violin. Many of the prisoners who also brought their instruments formed an orchestra of sorts. On Sunday evenings, there is a performance which is attended by everyone in the camp, especially the guards who naturally get to sit on chairs. There is even a small theater group, which is likely just a distraction for the prisoners. I imagine it keeps them calm and occupied just another way to keep life as normal as possible. It keeps everyone hoping that the bad rumors are not true. Stories, games, and craft activities help keep the youngest children occupied. The older children have classes a few times per week.

Rabbi Cohen—do you remember him from our visit to Amsterdam—has also been deported to Westerbork. Have you heard? He is allowed to conduct Shabbat services there. I guess now that everyone is together and jailed, the guards do not care what Jews do in their free time.

I would write to Sara but do not have her address now that you have all been displaced. We cannot forget the images of the destruction. Our lovely old city is no more. We are just grateful that your family is still safe.

Have you finished knitting the dress for Clara? We have a lovely yarn shop nearby, which you would love! Soon I will send some white yarn, shorn, carded, and spun from local wool. It should make a very nice little sweater to wear over her dresses, with spring coming to Holland soon. Enjoy your outings to your park. We understand that you now have to venture out without Mau, so be cautious. I know Jewish men cannot take a chance to be seen on the street. Beware of misguided people. Please be careful and write again soon.

Love,

Your cousin Alice

....

Rotterdam, 30 June 1942

Hello Alice,

It is a perfect afternoon to knit but I will write you first. All I have left to do are the sleeves for Clara's dress. They will be short so that it will be easy to pop on her little vest since it can still be a bit chilly here.

Life is becoming so grim. As I feared, we are now required to wear the Star of David. The Germans are continuing to isolate and humiliate us. They are also confiscating our bicycles because they need the metal and the tires for the war. Can you imagine that we have to do without them so bullets and other ammunition can be made from our possessions? The baby carriage you left with us is our only set of wheels.

As of today, we are under curfew from 8PM until 6 AM. We walk to the shops that will still trade with us, some have signs in the window now that say NO JEWS ALLOWED. Sara has not heard from Schmuel since a postcard from Westerbork saying for her not to worry. How impossible is that! We imagine the mail is censored and he cannot reveal the truth.

Mau has been using his darkest paints of late. I don't know if they are the only ones available from your dad's materials, or if he is expressing his mood. He is working on a forest which looks like it is weathering a storm; the trees are bent over and look windblown. I am glad he has at least this way to dream, as I do when I knit. Also, he does not smoke his pipe when painting, leaving the meager ration intact.

The yarn you sent is just a shade lighter than the yellow sweater I made for her, so I can see how lovely the dress will be for our little one. At her last visit to the new doctor's office, they were not pleased with her development. She is frail. It is very noticeable with her mass of black curls. Even when we have extra stamps for milk, it is hard to get any.

Love to all,

Sophie

....

Rotterdam, 26 July 1942
Dear Alice,
The rumors are over, it is official! Beginning on Wednesday, all Rotterdam Jews will have twenty-four hours to report to Loods 24 at the Entrepôtstraat and board trains to Westerbork. We will manage, but it tears at my heart to take Clara with us. She might cry and we would be helpless to comfort her. That is one of the reasons we came to the decision to leave her behind. Now that we have made the decision, the prospect of our separation consumes my every waking hour. I cannot sleep; I weep constantly. The decision is painful, but we are desperate. By leaving her in Rotterdam, she may have a future.

We talked with Mau's dear friend Dolf Henkes about this a few weeks ago, and he has made it clear that he is ready to help. Mau just mailed a letter to him asking him to come and see us. Hopefully he will come before we leave. There is not much more to say, except that we wish your family a happy future.

Goodbye dear Alice . . . Love, Sophie

I was now fully in the mourning process. Then Cousin Leo came into my life.

CHAPTER 14

More Family

Cousin Leo

Not long after I reconnected with Beverly, I met another relative who soon became a precious help in finding my Jewish identity. Leo van Thyn, who lives in Canada, is a third cousin. Our paternal great-grandfathers were half-brothers. Leo's parents survived the camps, were married in 1946, and came from Holland to Canada in the mid-fifties. Leo and I bonded well and have an e-mail relationship. He is quite the family sleuth. He has been relentless in his search for ancestors and in his intent to connect us as a family. His genealogical computer printout is at least twenty feet long. He continues to uncover distant relations and puts us in touch with each other by mail.

A chill ran down my spine during our first visit with Cousin Leo at his home in 1999. When I jokingly accused him of staring at me, he told me that so many of my mannerisms and body language reminded him of his recently deceased dad. Leo wrote this after meeting me.

July 1999

In 1970 I decided to find out some information about my family. With the help of my mother I wrote to a number of archives in the Netherlands (We had come to Canada in 1957 and my usage of the Dutch language was beginning to falter). Replies came

showing birth, marriage, and death details of my grandfather, my
great-grandfather, and my great-great-grandfather. I even received
some photocopies of documents concerning them.

For the time being I was content to have that much. My parents
had always told me that I came from a large family, but I only knew
an aunt and uncle on both sides of my parents. Most of my family
had been exterminated in death camps. Being interested in history,
I had wanted to fit my lineage within the context of Dutch history.

Having other priorities, I left my search and also, writing letters
was laborious especially since replies took a long time and were most
often unsuccessful. In 1987, I noticed an article on the then-Mayor
of Amsterdam, Ed van Thijn (in the Netherlands van Thyn is writ-
ten as van Thijn.). Thinking that my name was rather unique I
figured he must be related. But it appeared that further genealogical
research would be needed.

In 1998, I once again began my search. This time, being some-
what computer literate, I knew the task might be simpler using the
internet. Also, genealogy was quickly becoming a popular hobby. I
advertised my name and that I was looking for family connections. I
found some interesting things but also unpleasant ones, such as long
lists of van Thijns and van Tijns that died in the camps. I noticed
in the Dutch-Jewish Genealogical Society that another person was
researching the van Thijns. I emailed her. Bev replied that she had a
van Thijn cousin in the U. S. who was looking for connections. She
gave me no name saying that it was up to her cousin to give private
details. She also sent me a rather limited family tree upon which I
recognized no one.

Shortly thereafter I received an email from Sonja in which she
told me a little about her history. Sonja, Bev, and I emailed each
other for quite a while but we were no closer to finding an actual
link between us. In my search for family, I managed to get the help of
some very kind people – Marion and Tsvi in Holland and Marina in
Waterloo, Ontario. Marion visited the Amsterdam Archives regularly

since she was doing other genealogical research. After her second visit on my behalf, she sent me information that proved that Sonja and I were cousins. Again, I was delirious. Sonja and I continued to write addressing each other as "cousin."

Normally finding a cousin might not be such a "big deal" for people here. For me it was, since I had such a small family. Also, Sonja had a story. She was actually born as Clara van Thijn (which was my mother's name) in 1940. Her parents seemed to have some sense of what was to happen, since Germany had already invaded the Netherlands. Sonja's parents gave her to a friend with strict instructions that she be given to a Christian family. Sadly enough, her parents were taken to concentration camp where they perished. Sonja was raised by her adoptive family in Holland until they emigrated to the U.S. at about the same time as my parents emigrated to Canada.

Sonja and I continued to correspond and she told me she and her husband Ron were taking a trip to Holland to research her mother's side of the family. I put her in touch with Tsvi who upon her arrival helped her enormously. He wrote me that it was quite an emotional experience for her. At one person's house, they found a document which had her listed as having died. When she returned she emailed me, telling me that she was coming to the Toronto area in late June to attend the wedding of someone in her adoptive family. Needless to say, I was very excited.

Last Sunday, a man and woman stood at my front door. If I didn't know that this couple were Sonja and her husband Ron—I had not seen any picture of her—I would have known she was a van Thijn. The resemblance to my aunt Sippora—my father's sister—in Israel was remarkable. After about 15 minutes of conversation she remarked that I was staring at her. This was true. I couldn't get over the resemblance and noticing that her voice had something of my dad's.

We spent about 7 hours together sharing stories. Carol and I took her to Solel [our place of worship], because she wanted to, and we showed her around. Living in Knoxville, Tennessee she had asked a local rabbi about Judaism. She had also asked me about things in our religion. You see, Sonja is a devout Christian who proclaims her devotion to Jesus. She had been raised that way and has two daughters (and three grandchildren) who have been raised as such. However, Sonja is interested in learning something about Judaism.

Sonja finds herself with a dual identity, a foot in each world. While she is impressed with the amount of statistical information I have found—my family tree includes almost 2000 people—she is more interested in finding out what kind of people her parents and grandparents were. Unfortunately, this is difficult since most of their contemporaries are no longer alive. I have about three sources I'm going to try.

Why has this meeting so profoundly impacted me? I grew up with stories of people – family and friends – that had died before I was born. The only way I knew them was through the anecdotes my parents told. It was sad somehow, and I realized later that I mourned for people I had never actually met. My generation has grown up with memories of the dead. The Holocaust is part of my conscience. I have to constantly remind myself that our religion is not founded upon that horrible part of history; it's founded on Mt. Sinai.

To me, Sonja is someone that has somehow risen from the ashes. I believe we Jews celebrate life and the lives of all who have avoided such doom. To me, Sonja's life is a tribute to the glory of God. It does not matter that she follows another religion. What matters is that she is alive; a vital being. She is someone that has stepped out of my past.

My search began years ago and I have been able to put my family in historical context. Like all history, the people in my family have become statistics. But they were real people with stories to tell. I am happy to know that Sonja and I are part of that history of real people. If I never find out about another van Thijn of the past, I am glad to know Sonja.

My First Seder

My first Seder was in Canada in 2001 at Cousin Leo's house, two years after I first met him. He invited Ron and me to their family Seder. I had had earlier opportunities to participate in the Passover feast, when Rabbis came to our Presbyterian church to conduct such a service. Those were educational, but I was intentionally absent. That was not very gracious of me, but I am Jewish and held out for the real thing. I knew many of the Passover customs, but did not know if I ever would be a participant in the real celebration. For so many years, I watched Jewish family traditions, but felt that I was an outsider. I knew I was missing something very basic, but now I was invited in.

When we were seated around Leo's table, I felt that I really belonged to the van Thijn family. I was now part of the family circle. We each had our own Passover *Haggadah* and were assigned to read a passage from it. Leo explained each element of the meal and its purpose. He signed the volume for me, stressing remembrance with the inscription, *You shall tell your child on that day.*

I felt comfortable having just met my newfound families. I did not want to face new uncertainties that were sure to happen with new discoveries. But once again I was prodded to continue my journey. Cousin Leo showed me his genealogy, which he spread over five feet on his living room floor. Then, after sensing my grief at the loss of my parents, he admonished me to move on.

Thanksgiving 2001

A small world became very minute when I discovered other distant cousins, Nico, and his sister Elsa. Their great-grandfather and mine were brothers, making us third cousins. Miraculously, Nico also lives in Knoxville! We found him simply by searching for the name van Thijn in the Knoxville phone directory. We were *Mishpocha*, which in Hebrew means family. At age 60, I was finally becoming part of a family.

Thanksgiving 2001 was very momentous. The cousins Nico, Elsa, Leo and I met together for the first time during this Thanksgiving weekend. To prevent emotional overload, Ron and I thought our first cousin meeting should be done in stages. Meeting Nico and his wife Bea was a bit daunting. Even though it took very little time for us to feel comfortable, we did not have the same instant rapport which occurred two years earlier when I first met cousin Leo. But I felt sure that when we would get to know each other we would become more like family.

Oma and opa van Thijn, Nico and Elsa's parents, lived in Shreveport, LA. They also flew in before thanksgiving. Both parents survived concentration camps, and their stories were taped for the Spielberg project. The six of us met to hear Elie Wiesel speak. The well-known author and Holocaust survivor was the featured speaker at a celebration to honor veterans in Pigeon Forge, Tennessee.

Nico's sister Elsa and her family were added to the mix the day after Thanksgiving. The two of us had e-mailed for some months, so it was a thrill to meet her and her family. We all met at cousin Nico's home. Bea, our hostess, welcomed us before we even parked the car. She had taken great care to see that we were all comfortable and especially well-fed. Elsa and her husband Jim and their three teenagers were expecting to meet only with Ron and me, but we provided an extra surprise. Leo and Carol who traveled from Canada were our house guests for the weekend and completed the party.

There were no awkward moments like the ones that often happen when you first meet new acquaintances. We talked and talked some more. I did more of the talking and Elsa who is a social worker by profession was the attentive listener. Since we had corresponded, we felt like we already knew each other. The conversation just continued our earlier communications. When her oldest son was a baby, she was told that she needed a support group to deal with the emotions of being a child of survivors. Being in touch with a support group not only helped her deal with current fears but I think may have influenced her career choice. What a lovely family, what an honor to include them in my life.

Nico and Leo are sports fans and that made for easy communication between them. I worried about their initial meeting, just like a good Jewish mother would, they enjoyed each other's company. Those two have built a relationship with sports as the mutual interest.

Elsa had heard some of my story, the child who was very wisely and bravely given away. Yes, my parents entrusted their 21-month-old first born to a friend before they boarded the train for Westerbork in the Netherlands. They never came back, nor did either set of grandparents. Elsa reminded me that mothers usually carried their infants with them into the gas chambers. So once again I came to the realization of how very fortunate I am to be alive. There is rarely a day that I take being alive for granted, and our visit certainly cemented this once again. Unlike Elsa who had benefited years ago from a support group, I had none. Living in Tennessee was not conducive to talking or working through all my unresolved emotions, because there is no survivors group. Most of the time there are still two of me, Clara and Sonja, both very thankful to be alive.

It has taken many years for me to forgive my Daddy for not hiding and taking a chance on life. I am told that he was true to his heritage and felt it his duty to step forward to be identified for transport. He must have at least suspected that bad times were ahead and reasoned that there was no good reason to subject a baby to whatever was to come. As I am making new discoveries, or as I say the yarn is beginning to unravel, he has become my hero. I want my life to be a tribute to honor his memory.

I grew up in a Christian family with no knowledge of my Jewish heritage until I was twelve years old. Although well cared for accepted and loved by my new family, the ache to belong in a Jewish environment has never left me. Throughout my life, I was strongly discouraged to think about or find out anything about my heritage. Yet for many years I have realized that I am certainly not just a product of my environment.

Even though our relationships are genetically distant, I believe each of my cousins feels the kinship. My joy of becoming connected at that point of my life is difficult to put into words. The Thanksgiving weekend certainly was a great experience and I considered it the beginning of a new venture. It was more than that, it was a discovery of who else I am. Perhaps someday, I will find the rest of me. I continue to read about the horrors of the Holocaust no matter how painful. I have also become better acquainted with Jewish traditions and worship.

CHAPTER 15

Imagining Family

Getting to know my extended family was a critical first step. Still, I was not ready to deal with the past suffering of my immediate family. So my stories became fantasies of how my family's lives would have been if my parents and grandparents had survived. The stories I imagined about my grandparents made me think of happy endings. This is how I imagined life for our family. I could not help but create stories of what could have been. My parents and grandparents did not survive the Holocaust. There are no graves for any of the loved ones I write about. In my mind, I needed closure. There is a Jewish saying that people are dead only when they are not remembered. Writing stories and remembering my family meant that they were not dead.

Grandmother's Locket

Reunion—1949

In a few hours I will visit with them for the first time. Grandma Sarah and Grandpa Abe are hosting Seder just like before the war. Grandma is easy to remember by the ever-present lavender scent and sparkling eyes, even after all the years we were separated. Although it has been years since my grandparents returned to Rotterdam from the concentration camp we have not been able to see them. Mother says that they are still distressed. Daddy says they are changed people. Does that mean my grandpa is not the same tall imposing bearded man I knew as a toddler? Mother has often told me stories of our times together. We had such good times.

After our Sabbath meal, the women rushed through the dishes; then grandma and I escaped the house. Daddy and Grandpa were dozing and Mother was reading a book or writing in her journal. In the fall we ran through the park catching falling leaves. It was important to catch one before it hit the ground. That, everyone knows, is the best way to prevent winter colds. Seeing how high we could kick the fallen leaves is another happy memory. When we went sledding, we had the best time ever. The old wooden toboggan never failed to give us thrills. I was so proud; we hardly ever crashed into the bushes at the bottom of the slope. Grandma was always such a good sport; usually we brought the little green metal pail. We would carefully scoop undisturbed snow and fill the pail. I remember the sweet taste of the snow cream we slurped and I hope she does too.

Grandpa was special too. He used to check his watch and all the clocks in the house by the rumble of the evening train, because the station was just around the corner. We could always hear the passenger train approach from a distance. When the huffing engine reached our station, he would snap open his pocket watch while we listened for all the clocks in the house to strike the hour at the same time. If the kitchen or parlor clock lagged by a stroke or two, he would correct that error immediately. Such is the life of a retired railroad man, he often told me.

The same train is bringing me closer and closer to the past. I am so nervous. My hands are sweating.

Grandmother's Locket—1952

She has already emptied two dresser drawers in her bedroom. Grandmother Sarah is such a frail little lady. She becomes agitated, mumbling under her breath in some foreign language. Finally, she finds it, safely tucked under a stack of neatly folded handkerchiefs. The passing of time has actually been kind to her treasure. It is a small heart about the size of her thumbnail. The tiny diamond sparkles in the center; and even though the passing of years has made her eyesight is a bit hazy, Sarah easily identifies the initials on the back of the jewel. Her fingers trace their two initials again as they have done countless times over the last decade. Her S and his A are woven together just as they hoped their young lives would be for years to come. Their happiness lasted for many long years. The summons was delivered on a sunny summer day. Just like so many of their friends, they were to be resettled and needed to report to the train station in less than 24 hours. One last night they loved. The next afternoon they stood holding hands in the long straggly line. While their names were checked on the long list by a young soldier. Fortunately they were allowed to remain together on their way to Westerbork and then Auschwitz.

After three days and nights, the train finally reached its final destination. Shortly after being shoved onto the platform, Sarah was separated from her husband. While she waited in a long line, she furtively removed her locket and put it in her boot. Abe had insisted she wear her new grey fur lined boots even though it was much too warm out to enjoy them; actually his advice might have helped to save her life. How could he have known that foot wear was just about impossible to arrange. When she reached the front of the line, another demanded her jewelry. The bands of gold were roughly wrung from their fingers and tossed in with many others in a tin basin. Sarah also removed the tiny gold rings from her ears. During the next two years she used every spare moment to protect her life. One of the first items she arranged was the long scarf of undetermined color. It was big enough to wrap around her bald head and kept her from freezing during roll call while they stood in those forever lines. So now she wore her little heart in the toe of her boot without its gold chain. The next month, her new bunkmate had an extra shoe lace. Sure it was brown and a bit greasy, but it was long enough to wrap around her hand at night. Once again she was able to make arrangements, which is the only way to survive in this cold and dismal place, and so it was arranged for a ration of the dry bread. Yes, her stomach growled, but then the hunger never left. That night she could once again wear her heart. It was hidden in her palm while she tried to sleep on the sour smelling lumpy mattress. Surely Abe knows she loves him dearly and holds his heart in her hand.

My Locket—1961

After we return from the jewelry store, oma asks me to bring out the porcelain tea pot." From earlier experiences that means we are going to have a serious visit! Together we fill the tray, including the red glass spoon holder and sugar bowl. The creamer was broken years ago when I was still a little girl. I still remember that scene! Then we rinse the teapot with hot water and fill it with a measure of loose tea, no tea bags on special occasions! We have some of her delicate homemade butter cookies. Then we sit in the parlor and sip some of the fragrant warm brew. "Now that you are going to live in your own home, it is time to entrust you with the locket," begins oma.

"This gold chain will replace all the ways this locket has been worn for nearly sixty years. When Abe gave me the heart locket, it had a chain much like this one." "What happened to the original one, I ask, you have always worn it on a black ribbon." "Not always, you remember how your opa Abe and I did not see each other for nearly three years when we were sent to Poland?" "Yes, you told us that shortly after the train arrived, you two were separated." The snapshot of opa as a young man has been on oma's night stand for as long as I can remember. He is smoking a pipe and leaning against his bicycle. There are other young people in the picture but I do not know who they are. In Holland the bicycle is not just a weekend commodity but an essential part of life. We use it to go to the bakery, green grocer, and getting ourselves back and forth to work. In fact it is the major method of transportation besides trains and street cars. "In May 1940, Holland was invaded by Germany and we were controlled by Hitler's forces. By 1942, all Jews were denied the use of public transportation. All bicycles were taken away, recalls oma. The

Nazis wanted to quickly immobilize the Dutch people. Our world suddenly became much smaller".

"How did opa get to his office?" I ask. "That became a serious problem, oma answers, just ten months after the invasion he was discharged from the company he had worked at for five years. Soon there was no money to pay for the things we needed to exist. We traded brand new linens and other gifts for money. Yet, after a while we considered ourselves lucky to barter just for our daily bread. None of our friends had jobs either. We all found ourselves in the same hopeless situation. Remember, oma goes on, all professionals such as lawyers, bankers and even doctors were left helpless. Jewish doctors could only treat Jews. Most of them had no money, thus no way to pay for the services. Maybe now you can understand that when we were promised jobs if we agreed to relocation, we believed that better days were ahead. You were barely a toddler and your parents struggled to care for you, because your daddy had lost his job. So we resigned ourselves to leaving our home and our furniture. It wasn't long after that in the summer of 1942 that our notice was delivered by a young soldier. The next day we were to report to the Rotterdam train station. We had very little time to gather together valuables. Your opa, practical as always, told me to wear my good coat and new grey boots. They were much too warm in July, but you know, it is a good thing that for once I listened. Keeping one's feet warm as well as dry was essential to survival at concentration camps. Shoes were one of the few things that could not be arranged in camp." "What does that mean, arranged?" I ask. "Just about anything could be traded for a crust of bread. That is how the gold chain that was originally attached to this locket became a source of existence for me," remembers oma. "When we reached Auschwitz, the soldiers demanded our wedding rings and whatever other valuables we carried. When my turn came, the locket was no longer hanging around my neck; I had hidden it in my boot. The chain kept my stomach from growling for several days as I traded it for extra rations of what was called soup and bread. The locket

was now attached to a greasy brown shoelace. What mattered most is that I could cradle it in my hand at night with the shoelace securely wrapped around my hand. I am sure Abe knew that I held his heart in my hand," dreams oma as she gazes into the distance.

The Family Dinner

The 'hooikist', the old-fashioned Dutch method for simmering meals, has been brewing since before sundown. Even though I am not usually too concerned with traditions, heeding to my grandfather's mores is important today. This means all preparations for the meal are done prior to Friday night at sundown. On that evening Jews welcome the Sabbath, a day of rest and contemplation. The preparation for this meal is no small feat for a new bride with limited experience. We are having the traditional chicken soup. All Jewish girls have some variation of their grandmother's favorite recipe, which they reserve for their 'bubula,' their sweetheart. Mine is not written in a cookbook. Hanging around the kitchen during those times when I was seen but not heard has made this one of the dishes that I prepare with confidence. The dish's fragrance tells me if it is going to be good. The challah bread looks beautiful, a golden braided masterpiece. Making the bread was the real challenge and took the better part of the afternoon to complete.

I remember coming home from school on Friday afternoons. Mother never needed to remind me to leave my shoes on the bottom step of the stairs. Daddy and I knew she had polished, baked and cooked most of the day. Coming home on that day was like being enveloped in a cozy nest. My first stop of course was the kitchen. After I plunked my books on the table my celebration began. When I close my eyes, I can still taste the sweet crusty roll which melts in my mouth. It was a miniature of the glorious loaf which was showcased on the cut class platter. Then Mother allowed me to prepare the candle holders, which she would light when Daddy came home from temple. First, polishing the silver until it showed the reflection of a ten-year old with unruly black curls and freckles on her nose. The new candles were in the drawer of dining room table where the crisp freshly ironed linen table cloth covered the long narrow table.

Opa Abe and oma Sarah are first time visitors to my home. I am nervous not only because dinner should be just right, but because this is their first trip outside their new home. After both grandparents miraculously survived two concentration camps they lived at a home for survivors; those Jews who were mere skeletons and needed nurturing learned to become self-sufficient again. It was not just their physical condition that needed to be restored, but their emotional stability as well. I understand many people need psychiatric care for the rest of their lives. Fortunately, long after spending several months in the nurturing environment of the home, my grandparents did once again become self-sufficient and outgoing.

They recently moved into an apartment in The Hague. It is just a short train ride from Rotterdam. They consider this their temporary home since Daddy tells me they are on a waiting list to go to Israel.

It has been long time since we were together. The good times are still vivid in my memory. I still find it difficult to believe that the sparkle in oma's eyes has disappeared.

It is growing dark. Soon the Sabbath candles will glow.

CHAPTER 16

Sharing My Story

The Hidden Children's Conferences

I learned that there was an annual conference for Hidden Children of the Holocaust. But was I a Holocaust survivor? After all, I did not suffer physically and was told repeatedly by my foster family that my life was good, and that I should be grateful for what I have. Still, my life was impacted by the absence of biological parents and immediate biological family. Even though my foster family had embraced and raised me, I had no history and no identity except through them. Now I yearned to prove that I was not just a product of my environment.

I did not realize how much had been missing from my life until after we arrived in Houston, Texas, for the Fall 2001 Hidden Children Conference. What an awakening! There were hundreds of people with similar experiences. There was no need to explain my background or reason for being there. The emphasis was on telling one's story. Mascara made a mess of my face; we all cried and laughed together. It was then and there that I realized I needed to embrace my heritage.

I wrote a brief entry in the 2001 conference's Memory Book. This was the first time I had shared my story:

They never returned

Even though she is just a little girl, she knows they are talking about her. After all she is no six-year old dummy! Standing on the street corner, the lady who is pretending to be her mother answers the usual questions. They talk about concentration camps. Are there any survivors? We don't know yet, says the lady. What are 'survivors', and when are her real Mommy and Daddy coming to take her home?

She wants them to touch her new soft white rabbit fur muff and matching ear muffs. Maybe the people think she can't hear what they are saying because her ears are covered.

The Fall 2001 conference saw the beginning of a new friendship. Ben Klein and I sat next to each other in the first workshop which put together survivors from the same age time period, and so we came to know that we survived in the same country and were born just a few months apart. More of a coincidence, my husband Ron and Ben's wife Rita connected at the workshop for spouses which was being conducted in a neighboring room. As we spent more time together, we learned that they lived very near our younger daughter Elise Chapman. As we carried on through the evening, one thing became clear: I would no longer disregard my Jewish heritage.

Today, Ben and I have a deep relationship, one that only the two of us understand. Rita is a lovely hostess and Ron and I are often part of their family celebrations. Ben is really the only person who understands my frustrations with my discovery journey, and our long telephone conversations have been very helpful. Ben was also really concerned about the fact that so much information about my past had been hidden from me for so long. "Now you know. You can't put the toothpaste back in the tube." This was a gentle, yet powerful nudge. Ben deals with his memories and pain in a completely different way from mine. That has not kept us from being *Mishpocha*. Five years later, Ben Klein—Yehuda, if we use his Jewish name—dedicated this poem to me as Mom was nearing her final hours in 2006:

We fight the final hours

We fight the final hours
I should have seen it coming

I could have done some more
Did I make the right decisions
Did I really do enough
Why does she cause this torment
Why can't she go to sleep
The questions are too many
The answers are too few

They fight the final passing
To live another minute
To breathe another breath
The going is so painful
The going is so slow
They are too scared to leave here
They are too scared to go

But death is part of living
Why can't we let them go
We can help them on their journey
We can ease them on their way
We can talk to them in silence
We have to let them go

It took a lot of courage after the Texas Hidden Children Conference, for me to let outsiders into my "other" life. I finally took this step in faith. It was time to honor my parents. Who would know that they had existed, if not for my testimony? Who would remember my three little boy cousins who were murdered during the Holocaust? Today, they are only names on paper. And who knows whether the story of the Holocaust's hidden children will always appear in history books? I now understood that I should not be silent. Survivors must tell the world. And I was able to reflect on my history thanks to the support of my new friends.

My instructions as a child and even as an adult were always to forget the past. I was told to be *flink*, i.e., to be brave, to not flinch.

I did not know that one needs to work through phases of grief. This phase of my journey allowed me to finally mourn my parents and other members of my family.

Sharing My Story

Back in Knoxville, where my family and I are members of Erin Presbyterian Church, and where I attend the Presbyterian Women's circle, our yearly Biblical study that fall was the Horizons book called *Esther's Feast: A Study of the Book of Esther.* I felt a kinship with this Jewish woman who lived a double life. My first talk about my secret life was a short and emotional presentation to my church sisters at the Presbyterian Conference Center in Montreat in 2002. I realized that if you don't know where you come from, the future is vague at best. My writings began to change.

In Knoxville, I belonged to a writing circle. In 2002, my friend Gabrielle who collected our writings, had the insight to know that there would be longer epistles. Another friend, Stephanie, nurtured me through my efforts to relive my life. They both suggested that I write about each day of the week to trigger my memories. Having written a series of pieces entitled "Days of the Week," I was getting closer to my childhood, but only to happy memories and a normal childhood. This was also a way to cope with pain. I still could not face the painful facts that had been half-hidden from me all my life.

Without these wise and sensitive writing circle friends, I would surely still be hidden, much like as I was as a child. I have chosen not to publish these "Days of the Week" as separate pieces. Instead, relevant passages can be found in chapter 3, Part III, entitled "My Friends."

CHAPTER 17

OWNING THE PAST

Hana's Suitcase

Embracing Clara and finding Schifrah took several years. Each Hidden Children conference I attended after 2002 stressed the importance of sharing and writing one's story. I still could not fully consider myself a Holocaust survivor and had little awareness about the trauma of survival. There were several years of self-searching and doubt. Did I have anything to share?

During this time, I came to realize that our grandchildren had a right to know about their heritage. How should I tell them? At the 2006 annual conference in Detroit, my younger daughter Elise and I visited the Holocaust museum in that city. I purchased a book by Karen Levine, *Hana's suitcase,* which was age-appropriate for Riley, her son and our oldest grandson. I was moved by the true story of a little Jewish girl whose identity Japanese children discovered. Riley and I read it together over the next several months. Riley's questions prompted me to tell him about my own survival during the Holocaust.

I still felt uneasiness and reluctance to reach my early childhood. I still felt that I did not have the right to call myself a Holocaust survivor. So I wrote short pieces in the allegorical style. Allegories, according to the Merriam-Webster Dictionary, are *the representation of spiritual, moral, or other abstract meanings through the actions of fictional characters that serve as symbols.* They were the perfect tool for me, removing me from the pain of discovery while expressing my need for belonging. The past was still too painful to be opened. I did not realize at the time that the allegories were my way to cope, my path to writing about my real childhood.

Paperclips inspired me. I had read about the Paper Clip project by the Middle School students in Whitwell, Tennessee. I also learned that students at Oslo University began to sport paperclips on their lapels during World War II as a sign of support of the resistance against Norway's Nazi occupation. Then, by pretending to be a soft ball of pink yarn or a rag, I came closer to confronting the past.

Paper Clips

I was made from a simple piece of steel and bent into a shape called a paper clip. I tumbled out of a large container that my mates called a drum. That is what we called each other when we were born, mates. Very functional, some of the older mates told us. Functional, what does that mean? Most of us are now packed in little boxes that are bundled together in larger boxes. Right now we are being shipped to warehouses. That means that all of us go on a long train ride on rails to a city far away from where we were made.

Most of us are eager for the adventure. We have been packed in a large dark box on wheels, a freight car. Across the aisle from us are boxes filled with colorful threads called yarn. They are very pretty and I was hoping to visit with one particular group of bright yellow stuff. I found myself growing a bit jealous of their bright colors, and I wondered about their function. I never found out because they had to rest since they all had another voyage after they left the train. They were meeting a group of long thin metal sticks known as knitting needles, with whom they were joining together in a place where people came to buy them and take them home! I do wonder what it would be like to have a home. Our destination is a place called Norway. I overheard this from one of the mates who had family members precede him.

Although our function is to clamp papers together, in Norway there is another use. We must be pretty special since some are put on coats and jackets. I wonder who started that custom. Quite a few rumors are rattling around and no one knows the real answer. One of the larger mates heard that they have a king who set the example. He wears one on his coat when he rides his horse through the parks of his country. It is to support people called Jews who wear another sort of decoration. I do hope to be worn on a coat, since I love to be outdoors and see the people. Perhaps I will then have a purpose like the yellow yarn.

The Tool Box

I live in a tool box, not a toy box! There are quite a few of us fuzzy hanks, spools and balls all squished together. Yarns are not the only occupants of course there are needles, tape measures, pins and patterns. Usually we are all stuffed together without much rhyme or reason. We don't mind the confusion it gives us a sense of belonging. All of us are after all part of her craft family.

We are often rearranged. It usually happens after she comes home from her guild meeting, whatever that is none of us really know. That's also when the new kids move in. We know they often just came from the store shelves. They are very quiet for the first few days, and the rest of us know to leave them alone for a while. After they are rested, we hear the stories of how they were stroked, fondled and finally deposited in a metal bin. One delicate pink spool was so frightened because she was taken out of her cozy bin with all her other pink sisters and dumped among big, hairy, dark creatures, which she only much later learned were yarns like herself. She told us that they all scooted around for another spell in that miserably cold and drafty basket. The next shock came as she was again dumped on a hard surface, the noise caused by some sort of bells was deafening. Some of us remember that feeling and can certainly sympathize. Thank goodness she then came home to us and lived to tell about the adventure.

At the same time some long supple needles joined us. Most of us are tall and slim made of various substances. These tools are nothing we have ever seen. They are pointed on both ends and call themselves double points, now that makes sense. What was most interesting to learn is that they are from yet another toy box. All this time we thought to be her only and favorite toy box. No, it seems there are more yarn destinations. Lanky, that's what we named the newcomer, says there are also many baskets scattered around. They have stitches on the needles; and are called projects. They are made in many shapes and colors. We hear that lanky has been part of a project. It seems she was used to pull some brown and green yarn around in a circle. Not all the yarn was used and the little balls are in that other bin. It seems that is where a multitude of other skeins hang out.

That explains a lot. Since I am the impatient type I often wonder if I will ever leave this crowded container. I want to become a sweater, a scarf or even some warm fuzzy mittens. Now I know that it may be another long, long wait. Sure hope I get out of here before I become moth-eaten. That's another one of those human sayings that need some explaining. It seems that there are some bugs, called moths, who feed on wool.

The Yarn Bin

How on earth did we end up in this box? I sure hope someone rescues us soon for we are foreigners here. We are just two little balls of yarn. One of us is orange and the other has several colors strung together. We have been here long enough to meet the others. We all live on different shelves in a multitude of cubbies. Some inhabitants are sharp like needles and some others are made of softer materials. Nobody is as flexible and colorful as the two of us. Originally we were large skeins used to knit pretty garments. Now we are leftovers, scraps.

We are to be used with a blue gadget. It is called a spool and is running out of patience just like us. Our friend the spool has four little nails on its head. The idea is to wound us around these little nails and since we are so colorful, to make a pretty rope which will come out the bottom end of the spool. This activity is used to introduce little girls to real knitting. We really hope to be rescued before we are moth-eaten.

Meanwhile we are trying to learn each other's functions. Take these half circles. They live in pairs and call themselves dress shields. Unlike us, they are washable. They have been taken out and brought back many times to await another use. There are also threads of black, white, blue as well as pretty colors like orange and green. Their function is to follow needles through cloth: that called sewing. When the box is opened and a needle is selected, they all hold their breath, wanting to be the chosen one. Finally there is a round thing who claims to be very important! He is used to darn socks, what is that?

A Rag

A rag! That's all I am right now. It is winter and they have no use for me. I am tucked away in the garage, with my stripes all wrinkled. At least I am dry and safe from extinction for a little while. A month or two ago, they used me to collect the leaves all over the yard. I heard him say that they should get rid of me. Thankfully, she protested and said she would mend the tear that is weakening my spine. I sure do hope that she follows through. I have such a long such a long history with them.

I think it was within the first few years of their marriage that I moved into their lives. I was a brown cloth with stripes that were gold and purple before they sort of faded out. I was made of strong fiber and served in many functions. My first memory is as a bedspread; I covered the cot in their family room.

I do not know why she chose me, a nondescript piece of yardage in the fabric shop. I must have suited their family room. I was a mere remnant among dozens of leftovers. Ladies picked daily through us, the remains of once impressive bolts for decorating. We often talked about what sort of life the others were experiencing. Once in a while a lovely scrap would return for a moment. Their owner was looking for matching cloth, or someone had come to hunt for the rest of the bolt, which would also be carried away. We never learned why this happened, but we spun a good many stories about the life of those lucky remnants. We often talked about the day we would get lucky and move to live with a happy family.

I always thought it would be nice to hang as a quiet graceful curtain, blocking out the hot sun in some elegant dining room. There would be family dinners with children squirming in their chairs, as well as a high chair for the youngest, a chubby baby. I would listen as their voices mingled in happy anticipation of the next holiday. They would talk about the favorite dishes brought by the guests. I dreamed of rich cinnamon fragrance mingling with apples in the traditional cobbler, and of the hand-cranked vanilla ice cream that topped the mince pies. These were my daydreams for the future.

The Rag

I'm still here! The shelf where I was dumped earlier this fall has been taken over by Christmas wrappings. They no longer use the fancy white boxes. He fusses about them not being sturdy. So, now they use fancy bags stuffed with tissue paper to hide the surprise gift. The big roll of green tissue paper steadily disappeared last month. It I am glad it is almost gone because it has been cramping my style.

It is very delicate and a bit overbearing since it lives on the shelf with the rest of us rags. So we had to give it lots of room to avoid making any wrinkles in it. The other rags and I had to take turns moving about so that we would not damage that precious "green stuff," as we called it. I don't mean any insult. But my companion over there is a bit of a snob and doesn't want to be referred to as a rag. She is worn out and faded, but she is a sheet!

My temporary job has been to protect bushes from the frost during the past month. I was chattering in the cold. They were only concerned with some white flower bush called gardenia. I should not complain though, because once again my life has been extended. It should be noted that this family still appreciates cloth even though big black plastic bags show up everywhere. They are probably sort of old-fashioned since I hear that they don't like to waste paper or plastic. He regularly takes the newspapers from the shelf above us to be recycled. I wondered aloud what that meant, but then the cereal box that stays in the basket under the shelf explained it to me.

He and she reuse stuff, it is called recycling. For example, they started wrapping one Christmas gift to their family in the comics page. So now I know why the newspaper is safe from leaving the garage. They stay where they are until they are carried away in a box every once a month or so. That is what my box friend tells me. Since being here, I have become acquainted with objects which I imagine they consider as tools. The garden gloves, for example, have a lot of information. They go out quite often even on cold days, brr, I am glad it's not me. In the middle of winter they are used to help him bring the Christmas tree into the house. So they give me the low down on how he and she live on the other side of this wall.

Together

A very long time ago there were three of us. All of us were fashioned of red glass and embellished with silver. Our chubby creamer had a silver spout and sugar bowl sported a silver rim very much like my own lovely collar. We were part of oma's dowry and moved with her to many homes. Most often we had a place of honor, on a special tray or on a shelf. The high shelves were there to protect us from little grubby fingers. Our shiny red bodies made us a natural attraction for the littlest visitors.

The last time we were all together was when we resided on a lovely glass tea table. I remember it well. Oma readied the tea cozy and brought out a plate of cookies. The cups were lined up for the special brew when one of the little chubby kids who visited often knocked me over. All my precious spoons fell out and crashed into the creamer who toppled over and shattered. My sweet spoons all felt so sorry.

Right away I tried to convince them that they were certainly not at fault for breaking our creamer. After all their job is to stand tall and proud and wait to be chosen to stir tea.

After that incident I became very protective of my little silver spoons. Some of them were so delicate with their twisted stems. They usually sported an emblem or a flag of their place of origin. Several came from faraway places and often needed extra attention because their family setting was brand new.

Two recent arrivals told their sad history. They lived for many years in a dark kitchen cupboard, bored and neglected. Before growing old and tarnished they enjoyed being used nearly every day to stir sugar lumps into tea cups. They were used by two little girls who came home from school to enjoy afternoon tea and cookies with their grandma who lived down the street. Many special memories were made during those cozy visits. Sadly, it all ended very suddenly when one afternoon the lady was taken to the hospital. We do not know what happened then, said the little stirrers, but we did not see daylight again until we came to live here. We hope that visitors also come here for tea. It has been such a long time since we felt loved and listened to happy voices.

Witnessing

It took me a while to process all the recommendations I had received from my *Mishpocha* and writing friends. I felt the need to share my story with broad audiences. I was becoming increasingly aware that there were many other hidden children like me who do have a story and speak to civic organizations, church groups and students. After much deliberation, I decided to give it a try. My first presentation was in 2007 in the safe environment of my church. John Stuart, our pastor, and I used an interview style. With the encouragement of these friends, I developed a presentation which I now take to schools, colleges, churches, middle and high schools and civic organizations. After a couple of years, my daughter Elise convinced me to add pictures to my message.

There is now a PowerPoint presentation titled "Preserving the Legacy."

Since 2008, I have averaged twenty-five speaking engagements a year; I have spoken before school audiences in the Knoxville area, in North Carolina, Mississippi, and Kentucky. I have been interviewed and videotaped numerous times. Every year, I participate in the Holocaust Remembrance Day ceremonies on Capitol Hill in Nashville. I have been featured in and worked with the Tennessee Historical Commission. I am frequently on television. I was one of the survivors and liberators featured in the "Living On" exhibit that traveled in Tennessee and Kentucky. I became a docent at the East Tennessee History Center in Knoxville. I have donated artifacts to the United States Holocaust Memorial Museum in Washington, DC and have a recorded interview in their archivers.

Hundreds of presentations later, I truly understand that the past defines the future. To pay tribute to my family is an honor. Their bravery to leave me behind as they were sent into the unknown continues to humble me.

Racism has not died. Holocaust survivors are dying, but anti-Semitism is very much alive. In a few years, only one person in each audience may remember that six million Jews were murdered while the world watched. My message is to never be complacent or indifferent. Every person has a task to help fight racism. Racism grows in the soil of indifference and smothers freedom of speech. It is my sacred duty to tell you that "Never again," a phrase coined by Jews, can only be realized if *we* tell *you* that we will never again stand by helplessly, and that you must not be silent when you see racism occur. Often, we cannot fight back, but we can be heard. The most important message is, in the words of Edmund Burke, "The only thing necessary for the triumph of *evil* is for good men to do nothing." Silent bystanders always become part of the problem. I continue to speak, especially for the million and half children whose voices will never be heard again. My focus is on the intolerance and misunderstanding we have of other cultures and races. The most important audiences are students, for they are the answer to how we deal with those who are considered "different". They are also the last generation to meet and connect with a Holocaust survivor.

My text for life has always been "My grace is sufficient for you for power is made perfect in weakness." (Cor. II: 12, 9). It is because of His grace and the bravery of several people that I am alive today. My responsibility is to never be silent.

PART SIX

CLOSURE

CHAPTER 18

Three New Villagers

Josua

There are a multitude of Holocaust-related stories and I have read many of those. Why do I absorb all this pain? Has my heart become more vulnerable? What do I seek? In late 2013, my cousin Leo, forwarded Josua's story to me, and I have not stopped thinking about him since. Josua Ossendrijver was born in 1943 of Jewish parents in Rotterdam. Like me, his parents and his brother left through Westerbork for Auschwitz where they were murdered. Like me, he was adopted by Dutch parents, given the name of Klaas, and raised in Schiedam. Like me, he was given a new identity. He has written a book, *Verdoezeld verleden – kind van de oorlog* [Obscured Past—Child of the War].

I think of this man who has learned of his heritage at age 67. There is a connection between our experiences. He also overheard family conversations that did not make sense. Like me, he was invited to step into the next room with a coloring book. Why did his mother wear a Star of David? She was not Jewish. Why could he not attend summer camp? Why was he sickly, yet never sick? I immediately knew why: he was emotionally disconnected from those who controlled every minute of his life. Just as with me, someone tried to tell him more. It was an inebriated man who took me aside at tante Sien's garden party when I was seven years old, and whispered, "Mom and Pop are not your real parents." As our grandson Jordan used to say when he was little, "I already know it." Yet I still remember the chills running up and down my spine, followed by six more years before the truth was confirmed. Josua had a very brief encounter with a lady at a bus stop who tried to tell him the truth. He lived with his doubts nearly all his life. At last now I know the reason for my pursuit. Who else out there has had similar life experiences?

Like Josua, feeling safe to be Schifrah has taken most of my life. Until 2002, all my journaling was about other things—my true identity was hidden. I now know that this was my way of trying to please Mom and to be good enough, but I don't think that I ever succeeded. Sometimes I wonder whether there would have been more truth sooner if Mom had preceded Pop in death. Pop always seemed more open, less intent on keeping the vow of silence, less afraid to lose me. Also, why didn't I at some point force a talk about my life? Everyone has a right to their own identity, and although they were focused on keeping me from mine, I always was more than the product of Mom and Pop's environment. I long felt that I was their treasured possession and that they gave little thought to my emotional needs. I was not ever allowed to be angry or to be alone in my room. The gratefulness for being saved guided every moment of my young life. This phenomenon also controlled Josua's life, and it has deeply affected us.

Catherine

In 2013, Leo came to see me and asked one more time, Where's the book? I became earnest about writing approximately at the same time. At the Fall 2013 Holocaust Studies Conference at Middle Tennessee State University, I met Catherine Carls and started to tell her my story. It had been raining and I needed a ride to the conference center. Steve, Catherine's husband, offered me a ride, and Catherine and I started talking. We made an appointment the next day to look at my black notebook in which I keep documents about my parents' life and about me, pictures, and my presentation. Without Catherine's encouragement, my story may never have been written.

Linda

At the beginning of 2014, my voyage of self-discovery took a new turn. Just as I was ready to learn the facts and obtain the documents pertaining to the momentous events of the war years, about which I only had fragmentary memories, Dolf Henkes came back into my life.

In May 2014, while at my friends Caro and Hanno in Knoxville, both natives from Rotterdam, I met Caro's cousin Ankie who was visiting from Holland. Ankie is also a Rotterdam native and was very interested in my life story. In the fall of 2014, the Rotterdam newspaper advertised a special exhibit of Dolf's paintings in the Belvédère Story House in Katendrecht, a borough in the city of Rotterdam. My first villager, Dolf Henkes, lived nearby. Today, the Story House is a unique project aimed at building a community among the many social groups that live in Rotterdam. Ankie went to the Belvédère house and asked Linda Malherbe, the exhibit's curator, about the Schapedoorn paintings. Linda knew immediately that this was about Clara.

The puzzle pieces of my life that had collected over the years began to fall in place very quickly. Linda, who is a wonderful photographer, journalist and organizer, came to Knoxville in early April 2015 to find out more about me; she needed my story in preparation for the 70th anniversary of the end of World War II. She brought an amazing document with her: a letter dated July 26, 1942 from my daddy to Dolf, inviting him, his brother Jan, and his sister Marie, for one last urgent visit. For four days, Linda became my shadow. We spent every waking hour together, and while I answered her questions she clicked away on her camera with the tape recorder running. Caro provided the lodging, internet connection and other needed electronics for Linda, and drove us to all our destinations. With the tape recorder and the camera. Thus I was featured at the Belvédère Story House retrospective of one of Rotterdam's most distinguished artists. When I viewed the exhibit in 2015, I marveled at the result of the many hours of work that Linda and Joop Reijngoud, co-creator of the exhibition, spent to bring the month-long display into being. I was told that the top floor of the Belvédère house was used as a temporary hiding place during the war. Could I have been in the very same building in 1942 and again 73 years later to visit the exhibition portraying my life? How remarkable is that!

CHAPTER 19

Return to Rotterdam

It was shortly before Linda's visit that I was invited to participate in the events of the 70th commemoration of the end of World War II at the Story House on May 3, 2015. I was to be featured with another Holocaust survivor, Sifra Dasberg, whose life, like mine, was saved by Dolf when she was a little girl. The community would finally learn not just about the artist, but about the man who was born exactly one hundred years ago that year. I was very honored to be asked. Caro volunteered to be my travel companion for that visit Holland. She and I had only a few weeks to practice our Dutch.

My Travel Journal

Monday, April 20, 2015

On our way to Amsterdam, we are experiencing our first setback. First, I awoke to thunderstorms. Then, the plane out of Knoxville was delayed twice. It now is scheduled to arrive two minutes before our transatlantic connection departs. Should we go home and try again tomorrow? That would give us a day less in Holland. I was already anxious and now we are waiting in line to see what miracles the ticket agent can produce. Taking out my knitting usually brings good results; perhaps another route will become available, let's think positively! We will know soon, Caro is next in line. There are at least ten bored-looking folks in line behind her. There are no airplanes on any of the tarmacs. Then—this is the plan: we are now flying through Munich. After more than seven hours on the road, we are only at Dulles Airport in Washington, D.C. We could have driven and arrived at about the same time. We should leave in another hour for our long haul across the pond. Caro is prepared; since we both will take a sleeping pill, we have dinner at Chipotle so as to not be disturbed during the flight. By the time we arrive in Amsterdam, most of the day will be gone. Dulles Airport is really up-to-date with charging stations for cell phones. Very few folks are turning pages like me; most are staring at their screens. Once aboard the plane, I look out the window. We are surrounded by lightning, truly a fantastic sight. Many passengers are taking pictures. We must be flying right through a storm, and there are more in the forecast. The flight is full, so writing in these cramped, half-lit quarters is a challenge. I sleep through the night, what a blessing. Except for misplacing my shoe, all is well. Perhaps the last leg of our flight will be on schedule; one out of three would be nice.

Tuesday, April 21, 2015

At long last, after 24 hours of travel we are at Klara, Caro's Mom, who lives in Ridderkerk, a few kilometers from Rotterdam. Caro will call Linda to check the agenda for the next few days. This means repacking some of my luggage since I will be in Katendrecht for at least a few days.

Thursday, April 23, 2015

Yesterday, I made new friends. Janneke, a volunteer at the Belvédère, showed me to my very comfortable apartment last night. Not only does it have all the comforts I need, but it is right around the corner from the Belvédère, another name for the Story House, which will be my home away from home. So very Dutch: there were lovely bouquets of fresh flowers in my room. There are fresh flowers as well on the tables at the Belvédère nearly every day. Today we visited the former head office of the Holland America Line (HAL), which is now the New York Hotel. We ate at its restaurant which is always busy for lunch. The only sandwiches were toasties, all other offerings were soup and open-face bread slices. I ordered fish, which included slices of salmon on cream cheese. It was so delightful that I will order it again during my stay.

The HAL has very special memories. Oom Ies Spetter was an executive in the accounting department for many years. He provided Pop with a job as ship carpenter, and he helped us with our emigration to America. Often, when Pop went to the office while the ship was in port, he would take me along.

Linda and Joop, a talented photographer, are caring guides and escorts. We are like the three musketeers and spend nearly every waking moment together. They are the creative artists who originated the Story House known as the Belvédère. Katendrecht is a multicultural community with many artists and foreign-born folks. Linda and Joop's creativity has brought many of these people's stories to life. They did an amazing job telling my life story with pictures and film. I do so admire their energy and dedication to the exhibit which finally brought Schifrah to life.

Linda and Joop also took me to Feyenoord – home of the soccer games. My grandfather Abraham Van Thijn had a dry goods store there. We did find the location, but it was no longer a store. Right by the street corner was the Feyenoord bar, an old and famous watering hole with lovely old Delft blue beer taps. A good bit of copper was visible and gave the place a warm and welcoming ambience. We went in to do some more scouting. The owner and his family happened to be there and showed us some historical documents, but we grew no wiser about the dry goods store. I learned that afternoon that eel, one of the delicacies I was prepared to taste, is now a protected species. Decades ago, I often caught them on fishing expeditions with one of Mom's relatives, my cousin Dolf. I rarely ate one then either, because Dolf made me skin my own catch. We decided not to visit Toepad where my maternal grandfather has an unmarked grave. Benjamin de Vries, my mother's father, was in the Jewish hospital when it was evacuated. That day, many of the patients were shot in the street if they were too ill for transport to Poland.

I am trying to regulate my sleep pattern. Each morning, I awaken too early to begin scheduled activities, so I make myself useful with some journaling. I am thoroughly awake with the help of espresso. No wonder folks need only small cups of that coffee liquor! I do not use the hair drier, the Pilates ball, or the microwave oven; being on this vacation means that I am answering to my host at the Belvédère. I had my hair cut before the trip, so it is wash and towel dry, a time saver.

Now is the time to start thinking in Dutch, so I can be ready for Eric Post. Tomorrow, he is doing a radio interview. We hope to conduct it in my native tongue, Dutch, which I have rarely used sincewe emigrated in 1952.

Friday, April 24, 2015

I need to pull out the agenda to remember what day it is. So many activities each day – I am in a whirl. Eric picks my brain for his radio program. Linda asks questions that the two of them have prepared. We visit the address where I was born and the last address of my birth parents. I have no recall of these places or of the deportation site on the banks of the Maas River called Loods 24. This is the very location where my parents boarded the train to Westerbork and subsequently Auschwitz. This is where many heartbreaking goodbyes took place in 1942.

In this very place, a stark memorial has been placed, the scene where family and friends parted forever. The little ones who were murdered have their names inscribed on semi-circular steel plaques. The children's ages range from a few months old to age twelve. These 686 children never returned! These poor little children left with their parents and were killed with them in the death camps. The youngest, a one-month-old baby, brings tears to my eyes. For a few minutes, I trace the names of some of the other children with my finger and cry, not bothering to wipe the tears from my cheeks. Did they come in strollers or by tram? Jewish families were forbidden public transportation, but perhaps the rule was lifted for this, their last trip as free citizens. Were the children eagerly clutching their dolls or blankets? Were they ready for an adventure? Or did they feel their parents' angst and clutch their skirts? Mothers could not leave their babies, not knowing what would happen to them. What a tragic scenario. Yet, was seeing them starve and cry better? The two horrors cannot be compared. I am in a daze and don't search out the names of my cousins, even though I know they are there. I just cannot celebrate the absence of Clara van Thijn's name from this memorial. If survivor's guilt exists, this is it!

Yet I do now reclaim my long-lost identity. I found Schifrah on the bank of the Maas River in Katendrecht. My sorrow sets the tone for the next few stops.

We return to Katendrecht just in time to go to the photo museum where 175 years of Rotterdam's images are displayed in black and white. It is a photographer's dream to have his or her work displayed there and our personal photographer Joop has several pieces on the walls.

Miscellaneous happenings, memories. I still love herring. I have not seen sugar lumps for tea. *Eierkoek*, a kind of sugar cookie that I once loved, now I no longer like. *Hopjes*, the famous Dutch coffee caramels, are still fine, and it is tulip time, so the fields are gorgeous. The espresso machine and I do not see eye to eye, I hope it is not kaput, if I add hot water I can live with the brew. As I am writing, I see the fat neighborhood cat in a window across the street. It is called so because his owner walks him on a leash for weight control.

Saturday, April 25, 2015

I visit Katwijk with Janneke's friend Coby who is a sculptor. This gives Linda and Joop a few minutes to finalize the exhibit that opens at 3pm on May 3rd. After the usual cup of tea, the ladies leave me to visit with Willy Vink and her husband Ben. Seeing Ben in his current condition is really sad. He has somewhat recuperated from his lung illness. Although neither of them smoke anymore, the damage has been done.

He needs assistance with every physical activity, from standing up to walking in the living room, he is so very weak. The only time Ben leaves the house is when Willy drives him to the doctor. Upon leaving, he and I hug for a long time; he says we would not meet again, and I believe him. We then visit the tulip fields, fantastic sites. I am pleasantly surprised that they are not wilted as I thought they would be in late April. Just like for our dogwood trees, the winter temperatures determine when the tulips will bloom. Although it is windy and cold, we take pictures of the neat rows of fabulous colors as far as the eye could see. These sites are more impressive than the Keukenhof whose imposing gardens most tourists visit.

Sunday, April 26, 2015

Today, I reconnected with cousin Rudi and his wife Mieke, members of my foster family. Growing up, I did not know Rudi even though he is my age. I was better acquainted with his older sister Corrie and her boyfriend Arie. Her parents oom Jan and tante Cor lived in Scheveningen which was a favorite place to visit. It was just a short walk to the boardwalk and the long pier. When the young couple and their dog went for a walk, they were persuaded to take me along. Rudi has two other siblings, Nel (married to Jan) and John who lives in Canada. It was not until Ron and I visited Holland back in the sixties that we became acquainted with Rudi and Mieke. We were their guests several times during our subsequent visits to Holland.

Rudi and Mieke drove me to their son's apartment where I met their two grandsons. After a brief visit, they took me to their home for a quick lunch. They must have been preplanned the whole day as we then traveled on to see tante Cor. What step back in time! Corrie and Arie have grown old of course. I would not have recognized them. They likely had the same experience when they saw me. They always surrounded themselves with dogs and this is still true. Mieke and I spent a good deal of our visit dissuading the big hairy mutt from loving us. Their only son, whom I was meeting for the first time, joined the gathering. In perfect Dutch style, we first drank our afternoon tea and then enjoyed our *borreltjes* (grown-up beverages). Our final stop was the Van der Valk hotel where we enjoyed dinner together and talked of times gone by.

Note added: I did not expect to see them again since they are going on vacation with friends, but I was pleasantly surprised when they came to the Belvédère later in the week.

Wednesday, April 29, 2015.

Today I met Sifra, the hidden child, the other person honored at the Belvédère exhibit. We met several days ago in Rotterdam for the first time. Riding the train, stopping at small stations, and rushing by railroad crossings, watching folks wait with their bicycles in hand, was exactly as I remembered the scene from many years ago. I absolutely loved the ninety-minute train ride to Goes in Zeeland. It was the first and only time I ventured out by myself. The only time I worried was when the message came across the loudspeaker to alert us that part of the train would be separated and arrive in Belgium. As usual, I could not understand the entire speech, too fast. All I imagined was being on the wrong path. To ease my anxiety, I spoke to a group of young ladies traveling together and they assured me that I was still on the right track. They even told me the number of stations we would pass before Goes. Meanwhile, I noticed how many things were the same as we passed by the very neat little gardens with minuscule tool sheds. I think these were started many years ago as public garden opportunities for those who lived in the row houses that are so common. They were also helpful after the war to supply much-needed vegetables. Being Dutch, you just know that space is used for the staple, potatoes. Wash dried on lines fastened to little balconies smells like sunshine, the bedding is aired from bedroom windows.

When the train stopped at Goes and I stepped out, Sifra was there. We hardly knew each other but hugged like we were *Mishpocha*. If you think about it, all hidden children have such awareness of each other.

Gabriel, her sweet husband, led us on a tour of the quaint little village before driving to their spacious condominium. Sifra tells her story to school children in Rotterdam, so I knew something about her life. While spending the day together, I learned new details. She and her parents were neighbors to Dolf Henkes; that made us kindred spirits, although her experience is very different from mine. Sifra was eight years old when her mother was arrested and deported to several different concentration camps before she died. It was midsummer, so her mother went to the grocer around the corner without her coat, and therefore no mandatory star. By the time she came back home, a Nazi soldier came to arrest her for not wearing her badge of shame. Sifra's dad went to the police station to find out the extent of the problem and probably to plead for her life. The answer he received was daunting. His wife would be released if he supplied the names of two other Jews who would take her place—or those of two people in the underground. The two names he brought to the police the next day were of course fictitious. This was discovered while he waited at the police station. They roughed him up and threw him down the iron stairs. As Sifra remembers it, he was bleeding and black and blue. That was the last time he saw his wife. The Henkes family urged the rest of the family to leave immediately since the Gestapo would soon be on its way for their arrest. Dolf and his brother Jan provided contacts for both Sifra and her dad. She spent the rest of the war with a lovely family who kept her safe in spite of their own challenges. The husband, who was director of our very popular Blijdorp Zoo, refused to display the signs NO JEWS ALLOWED. Soon a Nazi was in charge of the zoo and Sifra and her dad had to move. They both survived the war and for a time moved back to Katendrecht.

We had so much to share! Sifra has also journaled for many years and has very organized albums. After lunch, we walked about the village which looked and felt like a time warp, and where I discovered a very historical item. Since many people could not read about a century ago, apothecaries had the head of a foreigner hanging over the door.

His mouth was open and one could plainly see the pill on his tongue. I had not seen one in many years, but the village of Goes has one. Today, it hangs over a toy store. Most Dutch today do not know this archaic story. I also admired the little harbor in the middle of town; it makes the village unique. On our way to the train station, I saw a Hema, a kind of Woolworth's—it was a favorite during my childhood. I purchased the must-have handkerchiefs. I missed the 3:30 p.m. train, but it was worth it!

Saturday, May 2nd, 2015

The Belvédère is where my life story has come alive. The exhibition named "The Story of Schifrah and Sifra, an Ode to Life" opened today and will continue the rest of the month. Bigger-than-life photographs projected on the walls trace my existence from a twenty months-old child who was saved from the Nazis in 1942, during the occupation of Holland, to my current 74 years.

Sunday, May 3rd, 2015

Today I told my story of survival at the Belvédère. My American accent interfered somewhat, but after a few days of practice, I can speak adequately, even if it is challenging. I was humbled to have an audience who knew exactly what happened. Many of the listeners had also lived through the horrors of World War II as children. A big bear hug from a complete stranger – such was my meeting with Josua at the Belvédère ceremony today. So strong is the connection between those of us who have experienced similar traumas. No words were needed between us to feel like *Mishpocha*.

My journey to Rotterdam was made special not just by the old and new locations I visited, but by old friends with whom I reconnected at the exhibit. For a few minutes, Jacques Detiger and I stepped back in time. Such a lovely surprise when both he and his sister Hennie came to hear me speak. Our history goes back to when we were all in our teens. Jacques took a leap of faith and adventure when he came to

America. For a short time, he lived with us in our two-bedroom home in Park Ridge, New Jersey. He slept on the couch and, as he told me, with his feet hanging over. Being well over six feet tall, that would be so. He remembers those days very well and still feels grateful to Mom and Pop for giving him his start. Not only did they give him a bed, meals and encouragement, but Pop told him to go to the Holland America Line office in New York where oom Ies Spetter would likely find a position for him in the office. So, my birth family was in the picture again, and Jacques worked there for a time. After he moved to New York, he and I both anticipated his Sunday visits. I thought that the home-cooked meals were the only attraction, but it seems there was more! Our after-dinner walks usually followed the same route, around what we called the electric lake where I ice-skated. Little did I know that at that time our feelings were mutual, we were becoming more that casual friends. We also dated a few times when I worked in New York City. But a couple of years later, he was one of the grooms-men in the DuBois wedding.

Willy called a few days after our visit in Katwijk and told us that her husband Ben was too sick to be left alone. I understood that she would not be able to come today. I wanted everyone to meet her, because without her reaching out to me in 1986 when the newspaper article "What happened to Claartje" was published, there would be no Schifrah story. To my surprise, she did attend!

It was reassuring to have friends who knew Sonja and could now meet Schifrah. So it was with Nelly, who also heard the story for the first time. She is the widow of my childhood playmate and cousin Wim. We also had some time to remember years gone by when we visited places of our youth the following day.

Monday, May 4th, 2015

Today all of Holland pays tribute to those who died during the war. Flags are flying at half-mast everywhere. Rotterdam Mayor Aboutaleb is conducting the memorial service at which I am a "special guest." Participating in the memorial service is very emotional. I have cold chills; I do not feel that I am there. After the service, we march silently from the 15th century St. Laurens church to City Hall. Josua is there too for the Memorial Ceremonies, and then to see his play, which is being read at several locations. The church carillon sounds during the 3-block walk, it is chilling. I know that I am walking with the crowd, yet it still does not feel real. The whole country observes two minutes of silence. All traffic stops, including cars, trains, bicycles and traffic lights. I stand in front of City Hall for the laying of wreaths by city officials and support groups. Am I really here? Am I really experiencing this somber occasion?

Tuesday, May 5th

Liberation day is celebrated today with parades and folk dancing. That is my last day in Rotterdam and I pay final respects at the Children's Memorial by laying a bouquet of flowers. I am deeply grateful.

Sunday, May 24th

Back in Knoxville, the memories continue to come back. Mom's older brother had a son named Wim. As children, we were close; after 1952, we visited together whenever we were in Holland. Nelly, his widow, came to the Belvédère and we spent the day together. She and her son Wick visited the exhibit after I left, so I did not see him. I met him years ago, but our acquaintance was complicated. He came to Tennessee when Mom and Pop still lived in their house in Johnson City and asked to see me, only to be told that I was away on vacation. He asked for my telephone number, but Mom and Pop refused to give it to him, as they had done with my Canadian cousin John.

Wick wrote to me after his Belvédère visit to explain why the family never sent to me Dolf Henkes' 1985 newspaper article "Where is Claartje?" Rumors abounded after the article was published. According to the family, Dolf just wanted publicity and was not genuinely interested in me since he had left me at Schapedoorn in a chicken coop. As we know, my story was quite different, and Dolf made sure that I was rescued. How many people believed this rumor? Mom and Pop's relatives did. Wick's letter disturbs me, yet the puzzle pieces continue to fall into place, confirming the extent of the deliberate silence about my past.

CHAPTER 20

Dealing with the Evidence

After my 2015 trip to Rotterdam I became more curious about my early and apparently lost years. Wanting to contact the Jewish Social Work Agency in Amsterdam, I sought the help of Esti Cohen of the Survivor Children Foundation in Amsterdam. She found documents that clearly explained my journey during the war years. As a result of this research, two new villagers came into my life. One of them was Hanno Weitering, a good friend and trusted collaborator who translated these documents from Dutch into English and researched maps and other historical information. The other was the woman who risked her life and delivered me to Mom and Pop, Fie Hartog. I do not remember her, but we must have held hands, or perhaps she carried me as we traveled from my hiding place in Katendrecht to Ermelo. Fie was a fearless resistance worker who became one of my villagers. She defied Hitler and helped to save my life. I am so very thankful to her. The reports confirm that as a social worker she did home visits in 1945 and reported to the war orphan agency during my custody proceedings. Since the agency recorded that both the parents and the child appeared content, my placement with Mom and Pop was considered fitting.

The word "closure" never meant much to me until these discoveries of new facts and new villagers. They have helped to bring my early years into focus. As a two-year old, I was too young to understand the circumstances. The records show that at a future time I would be told about my Jewish background and given free choice as to which religion I would embrace! Yet in the Netherlands it was important to save a Jewish child both physically and spiritually. Thus it was not by chance that I became a Christian. Sadly, it has taken a lifetime of searching for me to know myself, Schifrah.

At last I feel whole! I am happy and liberated! Now I know that my parents realized that we would probably not be together again. They were desperate to find a safe place for me. How absolutely courageous! We separated even before the dreaded order came for them to report to the train station, what an absolutely fearless deed! It was likely just hours before the train departed that Dolf brought them the good news: a Christian family would take Clara into their home.

I understand why complete secrecy was necessary during and shortly after the war, causing me to remain Sonja. During the remainder of the war, the official version was that I was a foundling. The only records of my existence were new papers masking real names and dates! No one even knew how old I was, and there was no proof that I was a Jewish child other than my black hair and dark eyes that betrayed my true identity.

By 1943, the Nazis realized that many of the foundlings were in fact Jewish children. Many of them were arrested and sent to their death. So how did I survive being a hidden child living a NORMAL life? It took Mom and Pop's determination and bravery as well as many villagers to keep the secret. Sadly, that secret has dominated my existence for 76 years. Not until 2016, with the help of new villagers, did I learn about myself, Clara-Schifrah-Sonja. I am humbled! There were many people in the resistance who were actively involved in saving my life. The tragedy will always be that I never knew any of them.

The question remains why my foster parents did find it necessary to hide me from my past after the war was over. The many relatives who visited Mom and Pop in America, both foster and birth relatives, were always told that I was too busy. My phone number was never made available to them. The same occurred when my grandnephew Wick visited from Holland. I will never know how many others met with this excuse. Why did I not learn that my van Creveld aunts were still alive when we visited Holland in 1965? Was my great-grandmother's portrait which frightened me as a little girl still hanging over the mantle in their home? We would have been so happy to see each other. Why was the article entitled "What happened to Claartje" buried? This made our trip to see Dolf in 1987 secretive. It was the only opportunity to connect with my past. Did I not have a right to know my legacy? Why did the secret last almost my entire my life?

The latest piece of evidence to reach me was the eulogy given at Dolf Henkes' funeral by his friend Mr. Laven. This takes me right back to where it all began:

> *In the world war, he lost his one best friend after the other due to German violence. First Piet de Haan who as machinist lost his life at sea in 1942. Then Iz. van Creveld and Mau van Thijn and his wife. He took their baby and with the help of the four people closest to him [his mother, sisters Jo and Marie, and brother Jan], first found a hiding place at a farm in Borculo, and when the farmer got scared [he found a place] with strangers in Schiedam. He had to tell Mau van Tijn and his wife, but they were already at the Binnenhaven entrepôt in Loods 24 and would be deported that night to Westerbork. He was very troubled by the fact that they didn't know whether he had succeeded. I proposed to go to Loods 24, bypassing several guard posts of the police and German police. We made it to Loods 24 and talked to Mau and Fietje van Thijn for hours. When the Jewish people were loaded into the train cars and had to leave their babies, we managed to escape. The trio [Dolf, his sister Marie, and his brother Jan] were overjoyed some time ago when a middle-aged woman from America, who had found out in Schiedam what the "Henkes trio" had done for her as baby, came to thank them for what they had done.*

CHAPTER 21

Goodbye Dear Ones

To My Parents

July 2014

Dear Parents,

This letter to you has been on my mind for a very long time. It is impossible to express my gratitude to you, Mother and Daddy, for the very wise and unselfish gift of life you granted me so many years ago. When I was much younger, I did not understand your sacrifice. Mom and Pop who became my foster parents and took care of me for the rest of their life, told me my true name was Clara van Thijn. I was told that since I did not remember either of you it was best that I forget my early years. I did that for a long time. Still I worried, why did you abandon me, should the three of us have hidden? Why did you not take a chance to live, after all you were not even twenty-nine years old and had a whole lifetime in front of you! It took many years for me to understand that your decision was a necessity.

It was a long sixty years later that I first saw your photo and thus you both became real people. I did indeed have a real Mother and Daddy! I have no idea when I chose these names for you. Could I talk as a toddler, what did I call you? You made some very smart choices by entrusting me to Dolf Henkes. It was only recently that I learned of his loyalty. He traveled with me for three days begging for a hiding place. It seems all his contacts decided that a toddler who might cry would be a hazard. The place where he was finally successful turned out to be inappropriate for a toddler. What anxious hours you must have lived while making the decision to leave me behind. I am so sorry to say that Dolf never received much gratitude. You see, I never knew that he played such a vital part in my survival. I always thought our parting was decided at the last moment; that in itself is difficult. Knowing that you planned this in advance must have been so painful for you both, like a ticking time bomb. Dolf finally decided to take me home with him; while his sister Marie cared for me, another home was found. I may never know how the transfer was done. Your red and black bead necklace was in Marie's possession for about thirty years. They did not know if my initial foster home would be a good fit, so she must have kept it behind until we met again. In August of the year you left, I came to live with Mom and Pop, they cared for me the rest of their lives. There were never any answers to my questions about my heritage. When my family was grown and I could finally concentrate on my history, I was determined to find out more about my early life and so Alice came into being for me. You remember that Daddy's cousin, aunt Alice, uncle Steven and baby Jocelyn left Holland just in time. After I learned that Alice knew both of you, she has talked to me about you. That is how Daddy became real for me. In the only photograph I have of you both, Daddy looks at Mother adoringly. Now I also know that you loved each other very much. What generous and selfless and brave parents I had! I will always be proud of you. Although there is not even a grave for any of our family, I do have a way to think of you! The Knoxville mayor had a large memorial stone erected in one of our city parks to honor the six million who died and those soldiers who liberated the concentration camps. Whenever I walk there, I always stop and put a stone on what I must consider your resting place.

My responsibility is to tell future adults that the Holocaust did happen and that I am alive because you gave me up. I want to be worthy of your sacrifice.

Much love to you both,
Schifrah

To Dolf

July 2014

Dear Dolf,

We must have looked like a strange pair. You were a tall slim man in your thirties and I was a dark-haired toddler. Did you have a stroller or did you carry me—for I could not have walked through the Achterhoek as a twenty-two month old! I was too young to realize what was happening, but for you it must have been an emotional journey. Did we start our search for my shelter immediately after you said farewell to your friends Mau and Sophie? Where did we sleep those first few days? How did you come to know Mau? I know he also painted pictures. Did you learn about each other through that venue, and discussed your passions for art? I am glad you were good friends, for my parents certainly would not entrust me to just an acquaintance. You certainly were prudent with the money Daddy gave you. It seems you spent a minimum and saved the bulk until you gave it to my foster parents after the war. How discouraged you must have been when no one dared to take me in? You probably became angry and impatient as well. So, you cannot be blamed for finally leaving me at this less than comfortable farm. Thank goodness, I can't remember those few days either. So it was predestined that you returned and took me home to your sister Marie. Although your home was surely not equipped to take in a small child, your sister and brother Jan rose to the occasion.

I understand and remember hearing that you were snubbed. One time I heard Mom say that she would call the police if you came near me. Why, all you cared about was my safety! The fact that you lived in Katendrecht, not the most savory neighborhood with the sailors, prostitutes, and artists, did not help. Regular folks, whatever that means, did not endorse that community, or those who lived there. All I can recall is that I left in a small tug boat with black smoke floating overhead. You watched from a distance; yes, I knew it was you or someone who did not want to be seen, when you were handed my school picture.

The same photo was printed in the newspaper almost a lifetime later. When an envelope was passed over the wooden fence surrounding the playground, instinctively I knew it concerned me.

Another connection, your artwork was visible shortly after the war in Rotterdam. I saw your paintings on my way to the movie theater. The walls of corner market stores called *noodwinkels* were painted with the same bright colors you used in your paintings. How did I know about the colors? It must have been that extra sense that drew me to you. But it is like the newsreels—I will never know why the newsreels were thought to be appropriate for me to watch. I always see those black and white images, people pressed against fences that remind me of metal cages – but only through hindsight do I now know what I was seeing. One should never ever underestimate the intelligence of a child.

When the preschool picture was publicized in 1986 with the article in which you were asking what had become of Claartje, I started my discovery journey. It was through the loyalty of my lifelong friend Willy that the article "What has become of Claartje" arrived in my mailbox. You must have known that everyone and everything related to my birth remained secret. But I was blessed with true friends who helped me put some of the puzzle pieces into place, even when facing the truth was difficult. You and I had a brief visit the following summer. I came to tea and we retired to your studio. I am sure I offended you when I rejected your gift of a painting. Please know that I have often regretted that decision which can never be adequately explained. I remember too that Marie gave me Mother's precious Jerusalem beads that she had saved for so many years. Did you keep them because you were not sure if Mom and Pop would be a successful match? Mother's beads were your last physical tie to the van Thijns.

It is much too late to acknowledge your loyalty and kindness, but I trust that you rest with the confidence of being my first friend.

Clara

To Mom and Pop

December 2018

Dear Mom and Pop,

When you decided to take me into your family, did you even stop to think about the dangers? Was the need to have a baby so strong that the possibility of being seen protecting a Jewish child could not discourage you? That was a real danger. In those early years of the war, being a foundling was feasible and you did just that, by registering me as such.

Becoming instant parents to a little girl could not have been easy for either of us. As a small child who had lived with many uncertainties, this must have been another strange experience. Did it take a while for all of us to be comfortable with each other?

I have spent most of my life finding out who else I am, a Holocaust survivor. I have been hidden for over seventy years. Thank you for loving and protecting me in your own fashion. I have now come full circle not denying my Christianity while embracing my Jewish roots.

I hope you both rest in peace!

Love … Sonja

....

To Riley

December 2018

Dear Riley,

Many years ago, when you were in the fifth grade, we began talking about your heritage and the fact that I am a Holocaust survivor. We eased into that grim subject by reading *Hana's Suitcase*, a story about a little girl who survived the Second World War. We took turns reading several pages at a time when we came to visit you in Georgia. It took us several months. You knew that I too was a Holocaust survivor who lived in the Netherlands during my early years. The story prompted many questions and brought us closer to discussing my life as a Hidden Child.

That was also the time we visited the "Living On" exhibit at the Knoxville Historical Museum. Your cousin Emily joined us to see the portraits of other Tennessee survivors.

Soon after that, I talked to your class. This was the most poignant and difficult lecture. As I looked at you in that classroom, I felt tears burning my eyes. After all, I barely escaped the Nazi terror, and there you were, my firstborn grandson! What a miracle. . . I will never take our lives for granted. Suddenly, I realized that I am the matriarch of a new family. I have the responsibility to speak to many audiences about the horrors that nearly wiped out the entire Jewish race, and about my parents who bravely left me behind.

It is a well-known saying that evil grows when good people do nothing.

Let us not be indifferent to racism, and I hope that you will tell our family of their Jewish heritage when I am gone.

Love you lots . . . Oma

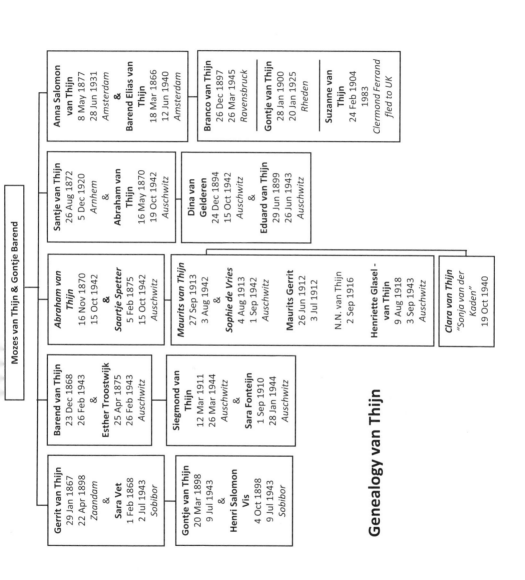

Genealogy van Thijn

Mozes van Thijn & Gontje Barend

Gerrit van Thijn
29 Jan 1867
22 Apr 1898
Zaandam
&
Sara Vet
1 Feb 1868
2 Jul 1943
Sobibor

Gontje van Thijn
20 Mar 1898
9 Jul 1943
&
Henri Salomon
Vis
4 Oct 1898
9 Jul 1943
Sobibor

Barend van Thijn
23 Dec 1868
26 Feb 1943
&
Esther Troostwijk
25 Apr 1875
26 Feb 1943
Auschwitz

Siegmond van
Thijn
12 Mar 1911
26 Mar 1944
Auschwitz
&
Sara Fonteijn
1 Sep 1910
28 Jan 1944
Auschwitz

Abraham van
Thijn
16 Nov 1870
15 Oct 1942
&
Saartje Spetter
5 Feb 1875
15 Oct 1942
Auschwitz

Maurits van Thijn
27 Sep 1913
3 Aug 1942
&
Sophie de Vries
4 Aug 1913
1 Sep 1942
Auschwitz

Maurits Gerrit
26 Jun 1912
3 Jul 1912

N.N. van Thijn
2 Sep 1916

Henriette Glasel -
van Thijn
9 Aug 1918
3 Sep 1943
Auschwitz

Clara van Thijn
*"Sonja van der
Kaden"*
19 Oct 1940

Santje van Thijn
26 Aug 1872
5 Dec 1920
Arnhem
&
Abraham van
Thijn
16 May 1870
19 Oct 1942
Auschwitz

Dina van
Gelderen
24 Dec 1894
15 Oct 1942
Auschwitz
&
Eduard van Thijn
29 Jun 1899
26 Jun 1943
Auschwitz

Anna Salomon
van Thijn
8 May 1877
28 Jun 1931
Amsterdam
&
Barend Elias van
Thijn
18 Mar 1866
12 Jun 1940
Amsterdam

Branco van Thijn
26 Dec 1897
26 Mar 1945
Ravensbruck

Gontje van Thijn
28 Jan 1900
20 Jan 1925
Rheden

Suzanne van
Thijn
24 Feb 1904
1983
*Clermond Ferrand
fled to UK*

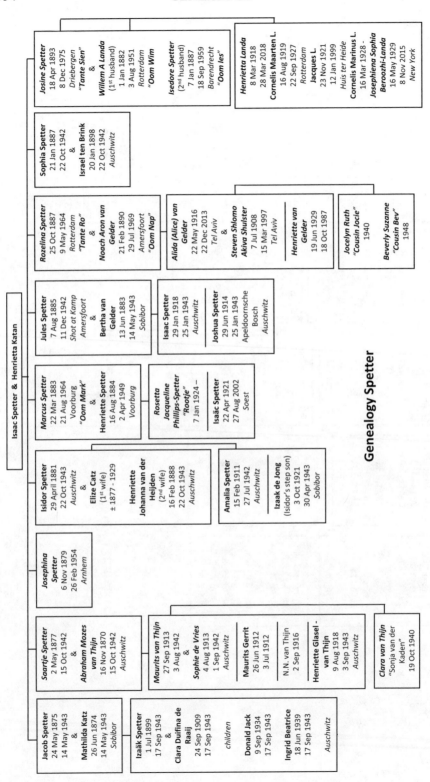

Isaac Spetter & Henrietta Katan

Genealogy Spetter

Josine Spetter
18 Apr 1893
8 Dec 1975
Driebergen
"Tante Sien"
&
Willem A Landa
(1ˢᵗ husband)
1 Jan 1882
3 Aug 1951
Rotterdam
"Oom Wim"

Isedore Spetter
(2ⁿᵈ husband)
7 Jan 1887
18 Sep 1959
Barendrecht
"Oom Ies"

Henrietta Landa
8 Mar 1918
28 Mar 2018
Cornelis Maarten L.
16 Aug 1919
22 Sep 1927
Rotterdam
Jacques L.
23 Nov 1921
12 Jan 1999
Huis ter Heide
Cornelis Marinus L.
16 Mar 1928 -
**Josephiena Sophia
Beroozhi-Landa**
16 May 1929
8 Nov 2015
New York

Sophia Spetter
21 Jan 1887
22 Oct 1942
&
Israel ten Brink
20 Jan 1898
22 Oct 1942
Auschwitz

Rozelina Spetter
25 Oct 1887
9 May 1964
Rotterdam
"Tante Ro"
&
**Noach Aron van
Gelder**
21 Feb 1890
29 Jul 1969
Amersfoort
"Oom Nap"

**Alida (Alice) van
Gelder**
22 May 1916
22 Dec 2013
Tel Aviv
&
**Steven Shlomo
Akiva Shulster**
7 Jul 1908
15 Mar 1997
Tel Aviv

**Henriette van
Gelder**
19 Jun 1929
18 Oct 1987

**Jocelyn Ruth
"Cousin Jocie"**
1940

**Beverly Suzanne
"Cousin Bev"**
1948

Jules Spetter
7 Aug 1885
11 Dec 1942
Shot at Kamp
Amersfoort
&
**Bertha van
Gelder**
13 Jun 1883
14 May 1943
Sobibor

Isaac Spetter
29 Jan 1918
25 Jan 1943
Auschwitz

Joshua Spetter
29 Jan 1914
25 Jan 1943
Auschwitz

Marcus Spetter
22 Mar 1883
21 Aug 1964
Voorburg
"Oom Mark"
&
Henriette Spetter
16 Aug 1884
2 Apr 1949
Voorburg

**Rosetta
Jacqueline
Phillips-Spetter**
"Rootje"
7 Jan 1924 –

Isaäc Spetter
22 Apr 1921
27 Aug 2002
Soest

Isidor Spetter
29 April 1881
22 Oct 1943
Auschwitz
&
Elize Catz
(1ˢᵗ wife)
± 1877 - 1929

**Henriette
Johanna van der
Heijden**
(2ⁿᵈ wife)
16 Feb 1888
22 Oct 1943
Auschwitz

Amalia Spetter
15 Feb 1911
27 Jul 1942
Auschwitz

Izaak de Jong
(Isidor's step son)
3 Oct 1921
30 Apr 1943
Sobibor

**Josephina
Spetter**
6 Nov 1879
26 Feb 1954
Arnhem

Saartje Spetter
2 May 1877
15 Oct 1942
&
**Abraham Mozes
van Thijn**
16 Nov 1870
15 Oct 1942
Auschwitz

Maurits van Thijn
27 Sep 1913
3 Aug 1942
&
Sophie de Vries
4 Aug 1913
1 Sep 1942
Auschwitz

Maurits Gerrit
26 Jun 1912
3 Jul 1912

N.N. van Thijn
2 Sep 1916

**Henriette Glasel -
van Thijn**
9 Aug 1918
3 Sep 1943
Auschwitz

Jacob Spetter
24 May 1875
14 May 1943
&
Mathilda Katz
26 Jun 1874
14 May 1943
Sobibor

Izaäk Spetter
1 Jul 1899
17 Sep 1943
&
**Clara Duifina de
Raaij**
24 Sep 1909
17 Sep 1943

children

Donald Jack
9 Sep 1934
17 Sep 1943

Ingrid Beatrice
18 Jun 1939
17 Sep 1943
Auschwitz

Clara van Thijn
*"Sonja van der
Kaden"*
19 Oct 1940

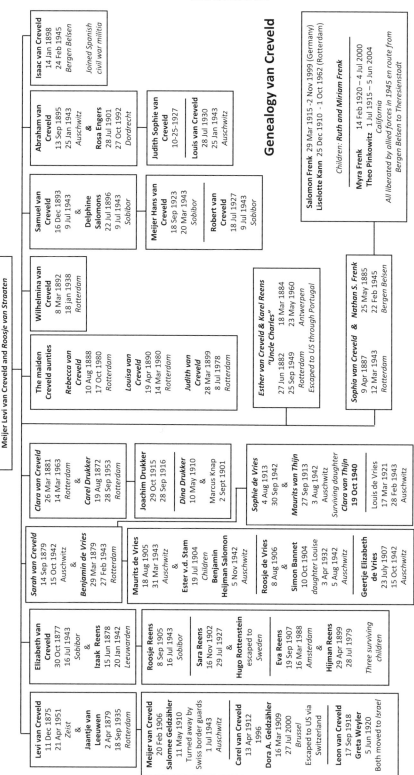

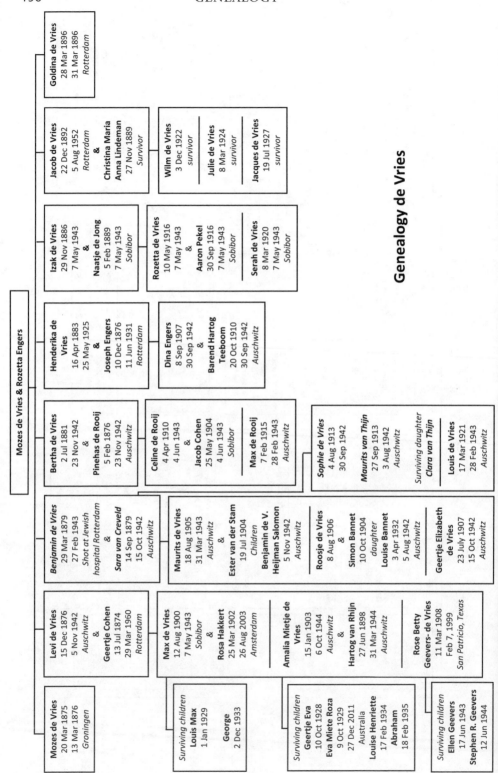

Genealogy de Vries

Mozes de Vries & Rozetta Engers

Goldina de Vries
28 Mar 1896
31 Mar 1896
Rotterdam

Jacob de Vries
22 Dec 1892
5 Aug 1952
Rotterdam
&
**Christina Maria
Anna Lindeman**
27 Nov 1889
Survivor

Wilm de Vries
3 Dec 1922
survivor

Julie de Vries
8 Mar 1924
survivor

Jacques de Vries
19 Jul 1927
survivor

Izak de Vries
29 Nov 1886
7 May 1943
&
Naatje de Jong
5 Feb 1889
7 May 1943
Sobibor

Rozetta de Vries
10 May 1916
7 May 1943
&
Aaron Pekel
30 Sep 1916
7 May 1943
Sobibor

Serah de Vries
8 Mar 1920
7 May 1943
Sobibor

Henderika de
Vries
16 Apr 1883
25 May 1925
Joseph Engers
10 Dec 1876
11 Jun 1931
Rotterdam

Dina Engers
8 Sep 1907
30 Sep 1942
&
**Barend Hartog
Teeboom**
20 Oct 1910
30 Sep 1942
Auschwitz

Bertha de Vries
2 Jul 1881
23 Nov 1942
&
Pinehas de Rooij
5 Feb 1876
23 Nov 1942
Auschwitz

Celine de Rooij
4 Apr 1910
4 Jun 1943
&
Jacob Cohen
25 May 1904
4 Jun 1943
Sobibor

Max de Rooij
7 Feb 1915
28 Feb 1943
Auschwitz

Sophie de Vries
4 Aug 1913
30 Sep 1942

Maurits van Thijn
27 Sep 1913
3 Aug 1942
Auschwitz

Surviving daughter
Clara van Thijn

Louis de Vries
17 Mar 1921
28 Feb 1943
Auschwitz

Benjamin de Vries
29 Mar 1879
27 Feb 1943
*Shot at Jewish
hospital Rotterdam*
&
Sara van Creveld
14 Sep 1879
15 Oct 1942
Auschwitz

Maurits de Vries
18 Aug 1905
31 Mar 1943
Auschwitz
&
Ester van der Stam
19 Jul 1904
Children

Benjamin de V.
Heijman Salomon
5 Nov 1942
Auschwitz

Roosje de Vries
8 Aug 1906
&
Simon Bannet
10 Oct 1904
daughter

Louise Bannet
3 Apr 1932
5 Aug 1942
Auschwitz

Geertje Elizabeth
de Vries
23 July 1907
15 Oct 1942
Auschwitz

Levi de Vries
15 Dec 1876
5 Nov 1942
Auschwitz
&
Geertje Cohen
13 Jul 1874
29 Mar 1960
Rotterdam

Max de Vries
12 Aug 1900
7 May 1943
Sobibor
&
Rosa Hakkert
25 Mar 1902
26 Aug 2003
Amsterdam

Amalia Mietje de
Vries
15 Jan 1903
6 Oct 1944
Auschwitz
&
Hartog van Rhijn
27 Jun 1898
31 Mar 1944
Auschwitz

Rose Betty
Geevers- de Vries
11 Mar 1908
Feb 7, 1999
San Patricio, Texas

Mozes de Vries
20 Mar 1875
13 Mar 1876
Groningen

Surviving children
Louis Max
1 Jan 1929

George
2 Dec 1933

Surviving children
Geertje Eva
10 Oct 1928
Eva Miete Roza
9 Oct 1929
27 Dec 2011
Australia
Louise Henriette
17 Feb 1934
Abraham
18 Feb 1935

Surviving children
Ellen Geevers
17 Jun 1943
Stephen R. Geevers
12 Jun 1944

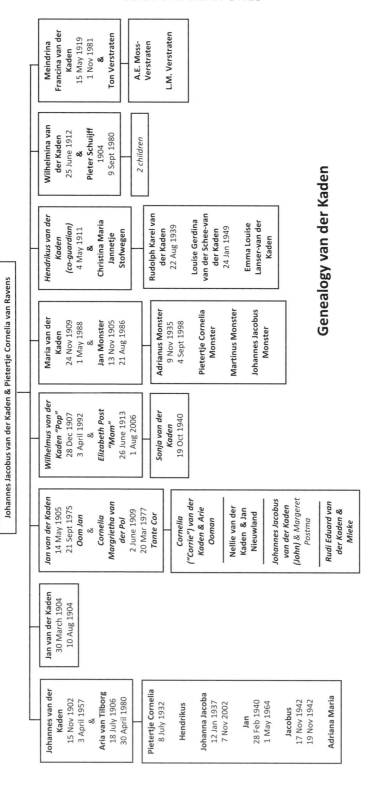

Johannes Jacobus van der Kaden & Pietertje Cornelia van Ravens

Genealogy van der Kaden

Johannes van der Kaden
15 Nov 1902
3 April 1957
&
Aria van Tilborg
18 July 1906
30 April 1980

Pietertje Cornelia
8 July 1932

Hendrikus

Johanna Jacoba
12 Jan 1937
7 Nov 2002

Jan
28 Feb 1940
1 May 1964

Jacobus
17 Nov 1942
19 Nov 1942

Adriana Maria

Jan van der Kaden
30 March 1904
10 Aug 1904

Jan van der Kaden
14 May 1905
21 Sept 1975
Oom Jan
&
*Cornelia
Margrietha van
der Pol*
2 June 1909
20 Mar 1977
Tante Cor

*Cornelia
("Corrie") van der
Kaden & Arie
Ooman*

Nellie van der
Kaden & Jan
Nieuwland

*Johannes Jacobus
van der Kaden
(John) & Margeret
Postma*

*Rudi Eduard van
der Kaden &
Mieke*

*Wilhelmus van der
Kaden "Pop"*
28 Dec 1907
3 April 1992
Oom Jan
&
*Elizabeth Post
"Mom"*
26 June 1913
1 Aug 2006

*Sonja van der
Kaden*
19 Oct 1940

Maria van der
Kaden
24 Nov 1909
1 May 1988
&
Jan Monster
13 Nov 1905
21 Aug 1986

Adrianus Monster
9 Nov 1935
4 Sept 1998

Pietertje Cornelia
Monster

Martinus Monster

Johannes Jacobus
Monster

*Hendrikus van der
Kaden
(co-guardian)*
4 May 1911
&
Christina Maria
Jannetje
Stofwegen

Rudolph Karel van
der Kaden
22 Aug 1939

Louise Gerdina
van der Schee-van
der Kaden
24 Jan 1949

Emma Louise
Lanser-van der
Kaden

Wilhelmina van
der Kaden
25 June 1912
&
Pieter Schuijff
1904
9 Sept 1980

2 children

Meindrina
Francina van der
Kaden
15 May 1919
1 Nov 1981
&
Ton Verstraten

A.E. Moss-
Verstraten

L.M. Verstraten

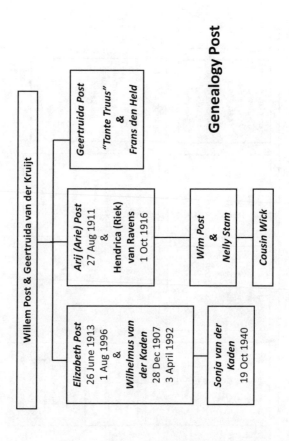

Genealogy Post

Postface

The following is a brief collection of notes that I prepared during the writing of this book. Some of these were initiated by Alice-Catherine Carls but were expanded after my reading and translation of the Dutch source materials.

Initially, the notes were an effort to put Sonja's personal recollections and revelations from the adoption materials she received in 2015 into a broader historical perspective, one that is factually precise and could help elucidate the course of events pertaining to Sonja's rescue and adoption. Much has been written about the May 14 (1940) bombing of Rotterdam, the German occupation of the Netherlands, the persecution of the Dutch Jews, the deportations from Loods 24, and the Nazi death camps in Eastern Europe. These historical events form the backdrop of the most dramatic and formative events of Sonja's life.

When we started the book project, we knew very little about the central figures in Sonja's early life. We knew so little about her parents, Maurits and Sophie van Thijn. We didn't know about the existence of Fie Hartog. Little did we know about other survivors in Sonja's extended birth family. What were the names of the aunts, uncles and cousins who perished? How was Sonja's rescue orchestrated and accomplished? What went on during the custody proceedings immediately after the war and how was it decided after the war that Sonja should stay with Mom and Pop? Why then did the van der Kadens emigrate to the US? To answer these questions, I needed to focus on "micro history". Such information is much more difficult to obtain. Typically, one does not find much information about ordinary citizens online, at least not of those who lived and died before the internet revolution. If lucky, one can find the birth and death records, though many records are still hidden for privacy protection. The only way for me to learn more about Maurits van Thijn was through his employer, specifically through archived Chamber of Commerce documents and archived correspondence between Arthur Philip & Co and the occupational authorities. Those documents turned out to be a treasure and shed some light on Mau's activities during the period 1939-1942. As I focused more on the relevant individuals, I did find some answers. Usually, the answers raised more questions, many of which remain unanswered until this day. Yet, as the project progressed, Sonja's narrative became firmly anchored to the factual events.

With the exception of the OPK documents (OPK stands for *Commissie Oorlogspleegkinderen* or commission on war foster children) and other documents in Sonja's possession, I only accessed material that is either available online or can be requested online. The latter documents were scanned and sent to me electronically by the Dutch National Archive. I did not visit any of the archives in person.

In an effort to best assist the reader, I interspersed the general historical and micro-historical information and placed it in chronological order, to the extent possible. This way, they best serve as the reader's companion as he or she finds out how Schifrah's quest unfolded. We intentionally did not insert numbers or footnotes into the main text as they would detract from the beauty of Sonja's writing.

Hanno H. Weitering
Knoxville, Tennessee
December 7, 2018

Notes

Maurits and Sophie Van Thijn.

Maurits van Thijn was born in Zaandam on 27 September 1913. He married his wife Sophie de Vries (born August 4, 1913 in Rotterdam) on November 12, 1939. The young couple took residence at Het Steiger 14 in the old town quarter of Rotterdam. A few weeks earlier, Maurits had started proceedings to emigrate to Great Britain, receiving a certificate of good citizenship dated October 26, 1939, from the Mayor of Rotterdam – a document that was required to obtain a visa abroad. On May 10, 1940, Hitler's armies invaded the Netherlands, and on May 14 the Germans bombed the city of Rotterdam, inflicting heavy damage, killing 800-900 people, destroying over 30,000 homes, and leaving about 85,000 people homeless. Mau and Sophie, already at the second trimester of her pregnancy, lost their apartment. They fled to Mau's parents who lived in Oranjeboomstraat, across the river, on the south side of town. They later found an apartment at Vierambachtstraat 66a, west of the bombed city center, where Clara was born on October 19, 1940. She should have been named Sara, after her maternal grandmother, Sara van Creveld, but since Sara was still alive in 1940, the baby was given the neutral name Clara, after her grand-aunt Claartje van Creveld – Drukker. Clara was registered with the Israelite Congregation in Rotterdam soon after birth. The letter confirming Clara's registration states her full Jewish name as Schifrah, daughter of Moshe HaCohein. The name Schifrah means "beautiful."

Dolf Henkes

We do not know how Mau and Sophie met Dolf Henkes. Dolf was close friends with Sophie's uncle and art collector Ies van Creveld, a leftist activist who had joined the militia volunteers fighting Franco's fascists during the Spanish civil war. Several other members of the van Creveld family, including the 'aunties', were known to be art lovers.

It is likely that Sophie and Mau, who dabbled in painting, met Dolf through the family's art connection. Dolf's little notebook indicates that Mau had bought or ordered a painting of the "Groote Schouwburg" (theatre) and another piece or art for a total of 135 guilders. They became very close friends.

Employment History Mau van Thijn

According to OPK documents, Maurits van Thijn was employed in the offices of van Creveld & Frenk, a wholesale company specializing in meat processing, as well as import and export of meat products. The company was owned by Sophie's grandfather Meyer van Creveld and oom Nathan Salomon Frenk, who was married to Sophia van Creveld. The company was taken over by a German (*Verwaltungstreuhänder*) in April 1942, practically meaning that Germans looted the company. It is not clear during what period Maurits worked at van Creveld & Frenk. However, we do know that he was employed by Arthur Philip & Co. from October 2, 1939 until January 31, 1941.

Our earliest reference to Arthur Philip & Co was found in an archived fundraising letter from the Jewish organization Keren-Hajessod, dated 27 November 1937, which identified Arthur Philip & Co., a wholesale trading company in animal hair and raw wool, as a potential donor for the Palestine cause. The business was located at the Kleine Johannisstrasse 10 in Hamburg, Germany. This was a time when the 'aryanisation' of Jewish businesses and Nazi orchestrated attacks on the Jewish population of Hamburg reached unprecedented heights. Aryanisation meant that the Nazi's robbed Jewish-owned companies and sold them much below market value to non-Jews. Arthur Philip & Co was formally disowned and sold on October 15, 1938, though it seems that Joseph Arthur Philip was able to pull out his capital just in time. He and his wife Maria Möller fled Nazi Germany and settled in Rotterdam on April 2, 1938. They initially stayed in a duplo apartment at the Rochussenstraat 85b. Rotterdam city records (*gezinskaarten*) identified them as Jewish refugees from Hamburg, Germany. The Nazis had stripped them of their German citizenship.

Arthur Philip registered a new company under the old name with the Netherlands Chamber of Commerce on March 31, 1938. Arthur Philip & Co was registered as an international trading company in animal hair, raw wool and related products. His business partner Hugo Moritzson from Hamburg, Hugo's wife Else Linick and their son Stefan Klaus Moritzson moved into the Rochussenstraat apartment on November 24, 1938, two weeks after Kristallnacht. The Dutch government was overwhelmed by the stream of refugees from Germany and Austria, and barred them from regular or self-employment. Many of these "illegal aliens" were stopped at the border and sent back to Germany. Others were sent to refugee camps where living conditions were often appalling. It appears that the Philip and Moritzson families were spared this fate.

Maurits van Thijn was appointed as the sole managing clerk and authorized signatory for Arthur Philip & Co on October 20, 1939. In this capacity, he handled all national and international correspondence and financial transactions. Soon thereafter, Arthur Philip and Maria Möller departed from Rotterdam and arrived in New York City on November 15, 1939. They stayed in the New York City area ever since and became American citizens in 1944. Their departure to the US essentially left Maurits van Thijn in charge of the company.

The business of Arthur Philip & Co was located in the iconic *kantoorgebouw* Hermes at Gedempte Glashaven 27. This building was completely destroyed during the German bombing of Rotterdam on May 14, 1940. On May 20, 1940, Hugo Moritzson dissolved the business partnership. He put his apartment in Hillegersberg up for rent on June 7, 1940, which seems to be the last record of his stay in Rotterdam. The Moritzson family temporarily stayed with Else's parents at the Pieter Nieuwlandstraat 79*bis* in Utrecht in 1941. Else's parents later perished in Sobibor in 1943. It is not clear how the Moritzson's managed to survive the war, but they eventually made it to the US in 1947. They became American citizens in 1952 and changed their names to Morrison. Their last residence in Holland was in the city of Utrecht, van Alphenstraat 38.

Following its destruction on May 10, 1940, Arthur Philip & Co changed its postal address to Vierambachtstraat 66a, the new home address of Maurits, Sophie, and Clara van Thijn. It thus seems likely that Maurits van Thijn handled all the correspondence regarding the liquidation and financial assets of Arthur Philip & Co with the German occupational authorities. While the correspondence was signed with "Arthur Philip", this signature doesn't match Arthur Philip's personal signature. Most likely, Maurits created this signature.

On or about December 17, 1941, Maurits van Thijn received a circular from the occupational authorities requiring Arthur Philip & Co. to report its United States assets. The circular followed Hitler's declaration of war on the United States on December 11, 1941, four days after the Japanese attack on Pearl Harbor. The company's response, dated December 22, 1941, was likely drafted by van Thijn. It was addressed to the *Deutsche Revisions & Treuhand A.G.* (a large German accounting agency charged with the registration of enemy assets and financial oversight of a *Verwaltungstreuhänder* on behalf of the *Generalkommissariat für Finanz und Wirtschaft*). The letter confirmed the destruction of the company offices in May 1940, the elimination of the business on May 20, 1940, the formal approval thereof on May 12, 1941, by the *Reichskommissar* for the occupied Netherlands (Arthur Seyss-Inquart), and the dismissal of all business personnel (including himself). The letter furthermore listed the contact addresses of Arthur Philip in New York City and Hugo Moritzson in Utrecht. It also provided a detailed financial overview with the proviso that the opening balance sheet for the liquidation phase on May 20, 1940 had to be reconstructed with the help of an external consulting agency because all company documents were destroyed during the bombing.

This and subsequent financial statements indicated an outstanding balance of 62,457 guilders (close to 530,000 Euros today) for shipped goods that had yet to be accounted for. In addition, there were two capital accounts belonging to Arthur Philip and Hugo Moritzson, which on May 20, 1940, totaled about 15,000 guilders with a 60%-40% split, reflecting their respective ownership share of the company. The total value of these accounts reflected the company's net worth. Van Thijn's report prompted the occupational authorities to proceed with the appointment of *Verwaltungstreuhänder* in an effort to locate the shipped goods and/or recoup the monetary value thereof. Mr. G.H. Hoyer, Burgemeester Meineszlaan 113b in Rotterdam was initially appointed *Verwaltungstreuhänder* of Arthur Philip & Co on June 23, 1942, and subsequently appointed *Liquidationstreuhänder* (liquidator) on September 14, 1942.

Van Thijn's final statement was dated January 20, 1942. It indicated that the net worth of Arthur Philip's capital account had shrunk to 2,028 guilders and 25 cents, which would be about 17,000 Euros today. That of Hugo Moritzson was in the red. Arthur Philip restarted his company in 1946 in Amsterdam. The company moved back to Rotterdam in 1949 and was located at the "Groothandelsgebouw". Arthur Philip N.V. remained in business until 1960. Arthur Philip died in 1977. His wife, Maria Möller lived to be almost 100 years old. She passed away in 2003.

Loods 24

Starting in July 1942, Jews living in and to the south of Rotterdam were summoned to report to Loods 24 for *Arbeitseinsatz* (or labor deployment). Loods 24 was an enclosed warehouse complex or entrepôt located at the Gemeentelijke Handelsinrichtingen in between the Binnenhaven and Spoorweghaven in Rotterdam. It was conveniently connected to the railway system for mass deportations to the death camps. Sophie and Mau reported for the very first transport. The first train carrying over 1100 Jews left in the night of July 30 and 31, 1942 for Hooghalen near Westerbork. From there, they were almost immediately deported to Auschwitz. Mau and Sophie were murdered on August 3, 1942, possibly later, but no later than September, 1942. August 3 was presumably the date of their arrival in Auschwitz, a few weeks short of Mau's 29th birthday, and one day before Sophie's 29th birthday. About 6790 people were deported from Loods 24 in 1942 and 1943; only 144 of them survived.

As can be seen from the genealogy chart, most of Mau and Sophie's extended family was murdered in Auschwitz and Sobibor. Sophie's father Benjamin de Vries was shot on February 27, 1943, one day after the Nazis had cleared the Jewish hospital in Rotterdam, where he was a patient.

Clara's Transfer

Details concerning Clara's transfer to Dolf Henkes originate from testimonies by Dolf and Marie Henkes, and from M.P. (Rinus) Laven's eulogy at Dolf's funeral in 1989. While there are some inconsistencies between the various accounts, they all confirm that Dolf went to Loods 24, not far from Katendrecht, on July 30 to say goodbye to Sophie and Mau, and that he was accompanied by Rinus Laven. Dolf and Rinus were lifelong friends.

In *NRC Handelsblad* of 28 October 1988, Dolf briefly referred to the events at Loods 24: "*I cannot tell what I experienced there that day, it defies comprehension. For a few days thereafter, I wandered around with a little girl that had stayed behind. The only shelter I could find was a chicken coop that belonged to a sister of a friend, somewhere in the Achterhoek. It is better not to pause too long thinking about this, otherwise you lose your grip.*"

This scenario seems consistent with Willy's account of her conversations with Dolf: "*Sonja's parents were afraid to get off the train (there were heavily armed soldiers near the train ready to shoot those who fled). In the end Dolf was able to convince the parents to entrust Sonja to him.*" Reflecting on Sonja's visit to Dolf in 1987, Willy paraphrased Dolf" "*It is not about whether they found us to be nice. I found out that I did not get her out of that train for nothing.*" Dolf's testimonies suggest that Clara was handed to him at the Loods 24 platform.

Rinus Laven's written Eulogy (see page 185) is a bit more detailed. It tells the story that he and Dolf went to Loods 24 to tell Mau and Sophie that they had found a couple that would take in Clara. Laven's testimony indicates that Mau and Sophie had entrusted Clara to Dolf well before they were summoned to report to Loods 24, and that Dolf's three day journey with Clara through the Achterhoek took place before Sophie and Mau commenced on their fateful journey.

It is striking that the accounts of Rinus and Dolf differ on this key aspect, *i.e.*, whether or not Clara was present at the Loods 24 platform. Babies were being deported along with their parents and one wonders if it would have been possible for them to escape the entrepôt carrying the little child while armed soldiers were watching. In this context, it is perhaps relevant to notice that Dolf's recollections in *Het Nieuwe Stadsblad* were not entirely correct. Could his memories have been mixed up? Memories do fade and both testimonies were made more than forty years after the event at Loods 24.

While we may never know for sure what happened at Loods 24, we do know that Clara was wearing a gaily printed little silk dress and a Jerusalem, red and black beads necklace when Sophie handed her over to Dolf's sister Marie. Many years later, Dolf's sister Marie recalled Sophie taking the Jerusalem beads necklace from her and placing it around Clara's neck at the moment of their parting. None of the accounts indicated that Marie was present at the entrepôt, suggesting that Clara's handover probably happened earlier. Marie's recollection thus seems mostly consistent with Rinus' version of the events.

Hiding Place

Dolf lived near the Belvédère, together with his brother Jan and sister Marie. Belvédère was a very popular café restaurant and jazz club, a place where sailors, immigrants and shipyard workers used to hang out. His fellow artist Valdemar Hansen (Wally) Elenbaas, a pre-war Communist who was forging documents for the resistance, lived there with his wife Esther Hartog, daughter of a Jewish diamond cutter. Wally and Esther were involved finding hiding places for Jewish children. Katendrecht was relatively safe because German soldiers were ordered not to enter this prostitution-ridden neighborhood, although house searches did take place. In 1942, Esther went into hiding on the second and third floors of Belvédère. Jewish children, likely including Clara, were also hidden there. Esther's sister Fie Hartog eventually took Clara to the van der Kadens, who then reported her as a foundling and were granted temporary guardianship. Fie Hartog later testified to OPK about Clara's rescue.

Belvédère is now a vibrant meeting place that brings together different social constituencies in Rotterdam. In 2014 and 2015, it hosted several exhibitions about former occupants Esther Hartog and Wally Elenbaas, their neighbor Dolf Henkes, and their role in hiding Jewish children, specifically Clara van Thijn and Sifra Dasberg. The exhibition was put together by community organizers Joop Reijngoud and Linda Malherbe. As such, they have played a key role in reconstructing Sonja's history. Linda kindly recovered critical documents from the Henkes archive, including Dolf's Eulogy.

Mounting Suspicion

After his disappointing journey through the Achterhoek, Dolf returned to Katendrecht and kept Clara in hiding for several weeks. He made an entry in his note booklet stating that he had spent 12 guilders on the trip. While caring for Clara, he scrupulously noted all expenses related to the child whose care had been entrusted to him. Mau and Sophie had given him a significant sum of money, about two thousand guilders—approximately $17,000.00 today—for her upbringing and care. They must have given him the money in cash, for he deposited nineteen hundred guilders at the Rijkspostspaarbank on August 27, 1942, five days after Clara was safely delivered to the van der Kadens. Even though Dolf did not leave Clara in the chicken coop and did not use any of Mau and Sophie's money for himself, he remained under a cloud of suspicion all his life. Many, including many in Sonja's extended foster family, believed that he had left her at the chicken farm and made financial gains from the whole affair. The family was scared of

Dolf because he was different, lived in a bad neighborhood; making matters worse, he was convicted of a stabbing incident in 1967. Similar prejudice may have been the reason why the van Creveld aunties urged the OPK that Dolf not be given any rights in Clara's upbringing.

Financial Transaction

Dolf received about two thousand guilders from Maurits and Sophie van Thijn for the care and upbringing of their daughter. Two thousand guilders was a lot of money, roughly the yearly income of a middle class family, and was not easy to come by. We do not know if the van Thijns had any savings or source of income after January 31, 1941. According to the OPK documents, Maurits and Sophie van Thijn had a modest income before the war.

Incidentally, the two thousand guilders almost equals the final balance on Arthur Philip's capital account in Arthur Philip & Co. It is not clear if van Thijn would have been able to access such a large sum of money from the company's bank account. Perhaps Arthur Philip authorized Mau to use the balance funds, or perhaps the monies came from Mau or Sophie's family.

Options were limited. By August 1941, Jewish citizens were required to deposit their money and securities with the LiRo looting bank, the counterfeit Sarphatistraat branch of the trusted Jewish Lippmann, Rosenthal & Co. bank. While the ruling initially applied to assets totaling more than ten thousand guilders, as of June 30, 1942, private Jews were no longer allowed to have more than 250 guilders at their disposal. Deposited funds were practically inaccessible due to regulatory compliance and high bank fees. Maurits and Sophie van Thijn also deposited some valuables such as a watch and ring at the LiRo bank, but they also left valuables with tante Sien and oom Wim Landa where they would be relatively safe, since theirs was a mixed marriage. Many Jews deposited only a small fraction of their valuables with LiRo, just enough to avoid potential house searches. After the war, it was determined that the van Thijn's LiRo deposits amounted to no more than 82 Deutsche Mark, which would be about 780 Euros today.

Eventually, the assets of Arthur Philip & Co would also be deposited with the LiRo bank, but not until a liquidator named G.H. Hoyer had been appointed. Thus, there may have been a window of opportunity for van Thijn to access company funds as Arthur Philip & Co came under Hoyer's control only a few weeks before Maurits and Sophie van Thijn entrusted their little daughter Clara and two thousand guilders to their friend Dolf Henkes. Regardless of how Mau van Thijn was able to access this much money, it appears quite likely that he had planned this move well ahead of time.

Willem and Elisabeth van der Kaden

Dolf's activities in the resistance made it possible for him to put an 'advertisement' in code in an underground leaflet. There were several underground organizations involved in saving, smuggling, and hiding Jews. Among them was the Landelijke Organisatie voor Hulp aan Onderduikers, or (LO) for Jews and non-Jews in hiding. Whether Dolf placed an ad, or whether Esther or Fie Hartog did this, is not known but a childless couple, Willem and Elisabeth van der Kaden responded. According to Elisabeth Van der Kaden, Willem was active in the resistance. This has not been documented; the only documentation possibly attesting to his role in the underground is a photograph of him in his uniform as a citizen's militia man, perhaps the *binnenlandse strijdkracht-en* charged with keeping peace and order in the tumultuous days after the liberation. According to OPK documents, he was a commander of a NSB (Dutch Nazi party) women's prisoner camp. National Archive documents indicate that Willem was employed by the Directoraat Generaal voor de Bijzondere Rechtspleging (General Directorate for Extraordinary Judicial Proceedings), which was charged with the formal judicial proceedings and prosecution of Dutch collaborators in the years immediately after the war. Willem was stationed as prisoner guard at three different prisoner camps: Bewaringskamp en Verblijfskamp (Arrest and Residence Camp) *'De Vlijt'* on the island of Texel, Bewaringskamp *'Fort Haerlem'* in Hellevoetsluis, and the Bewaringskamp en

Verblijfskamp *'Hulpziekenhuis Barkastraat'* in Rotterdam. Elisabeth van der Kaden had volunteered for the Red Cross.

The Parade

Sonja's memory about a 'Parade' of young men possibly refers to the *'Razzia of Rotterdam'* on November 10 and 11, 1944. About 8000 German soldiers rounded up through house-to-house searches about 52,000 out of the 70,000 men, ages 17 to 40, living in Schiedam and Rotterdam, to be sent to the weapons factories in Germany. At least 410 of them did not return. Willem van der Kaden escaped capture by hiding, though it was still very dangerous for him to be seen in the weeks after. Sonja's memories indicate she was living at the Overschi-eschestraat at the time she witnessed the parade, and that the weather was dreary. Both are consistent with the happenings of November 10, 11 in 1944. It was the biggest wartime razzia in Holland.

The Fate of the Dutch Jews

After the capitulation of the Netherlands on May 15, 1940, the government and the royal family fled to England, leaving the country to be occupied by the Germans who installed a 'civilian' government headed by *Reichskommissar* Arthur Seyss-Inquart. He quickly outlawed all political parties and 'nazified' the country. About 600,000 Dutch civilians were drafted or rounded up for forced labor or *Arbeitseinsatz* in the German war industry. The persecution of the Dutch Jews started almost immediately and was ramped up steadily. At the start of the invasion, there were about 140,000 Jews in the Netherlands. Rotterdam was, after Amsterdam and The Hague, the city with the largest Jewish population, numbering about 13,000 in 1939. About 1,200 Jews were evacuated following the bombing of May 1940, and another 800 Jewish refugees were forced to leave as well. By October 1941, the Jewish population of Rotterdam registered at approximately 11,000. These Jews were progressively and systematically removed from the government, the press, and business leadership. In February 1941, having opened several roundup places and transit camps, the occupation authorities began deporting Dutch Jews to Buchenwald and Mauthausen. This measure was met with a nationwide strike on February 25-26, 1941 – the sole protest of this kind in Nazi-occupied Europe.

In May 1942, all Dutch Jews were ordered to wear the Star of David. Mass deportations to the extermination camps started soon thereafter on July 15, 1942. Of the 107,000 deported Dutch Jews, only 5,200, or 4.9%, were alive by war's end; this was the highest death toll suffered by the Jewish population of any western European country. While aggregate statistics are relatively easy to find, reconstructing individual stories is more problematic. Dutch Jews were trying to avoid deportation either by fleeing or by hiding. Few were able to afford paying a smuggler or had contacts with non-Jews who might help them hide. Almost 1000 Jews were still able to emigrate 'legally' in 1940 and 1941 at very high monetary cost. An estimated 3000 Jews emigrated illegally and 25,000 went into hiding.

Approximately 36,000 Dutch Jews survived the war. Apart from the 5,200 camp survivors, about 16,500 Jews survived in hiding and about 10,000 Jews survived in mixed marriages. Over 3,000 were granted petitions by a German lawyer, Hans Calmeyer, to annul their classification as Jew or half Jew (Yad Vashem later recognized Hans Calmeyer as *Righteous among the Nations*). Others fled the country. Among those in hiding were Mau's oom Marcus Spetter and his family, who lived in Voorburg, and the van Creveld aunties in Rotterdam. (Judith and Rebecca van Creveld were hiding with the protestant Havelaar family at the Oostervantstraat 5a in Rotterdam). At the time of Clara's custody hearings, there were no known survivors of the van Thijn and de Vries families.

Commission on War Foster Children

This was the *Commissie voor Oorlogspleegkinderen,* abbreviated in Dutch as OPK. Among the roughly 4,000 Dutch Jewish children who survived, 2,041 were orphaned, and 1,363 were under the age of 15. While many in the Jewish community were hoping reunite their children with surviving family members, foster parents often refused to cooperate. Custody cases were reviewed by the government appointed OPK. The legal framework for the commission's task had already been conceived during the final years of the war by members of the underground and the Dutch government in exile. Board members initially included ten representatives of the Jewish community and fourteen former resistance fighters who had often personally saved the children and had placed them with their foster families. The OPK was formally instituted on May 8, 1945. The ultimate decision concerning guardianship resided with the courts, who almost always followed OPK's advice.

The government stipulated per a Royal Decree of August 13, 1945, that Jewish children hidden by gentile foster families would fall under the jurisdiction of the Commission if no returning parent had informed the Commission of his or her intent to claim the child within one month of the publication of the new law. In order to claim the children, Jewish relatives had to declare and prove the parents' intent to raise their children according to the Jewish faith. They were subjected to lengthy interrogation and extensive fact checking. Camp survivors were judged by their mental fitness and financial situation and were often deemed unsuitable as parents. In the first few years after the war, the odds were clearly stacked against the Jewish community, which in turn led to conflict among the Jewish and gentile members of the board. In this context, it is interesting to note that the wishes of Clara's parents that Clara be raised in a Christian family was later distorted in the OPK custody hearing where it was stated that Clara's parents *did not want their child to be known as Jewish.* Such a statement may have seemed plausible in the context of the situation in 1942, as the van Creveld sisters pointed out. Later, for the van der Kaden's, it might have been the pretext to erase all memories of Clara's Jewish heritage. Blinded by a mix of good intentions and Christian orthodoxy, many believed Jewish children would be far better off being raised in Christian families. The OPK board fell apart twice and was finally dissolved in 1949.

Custody Proceedings

Official documentation about the actual custody proceedings, obtained by Sonja DuBois in 2015, reveal a drama in three acts. The first act was the granting of temporary guardianship to Willem and Elisabeth van der Kaden on September 11, 1945. They had reported Sonja on April 13, 1943 as a "foundling" and were given temporary custody then by a lower court judge. Following the Royal Decree of August 13, 1945, given that no birth parent had come forth, they were again granted temporary custody. And on September 26, the Clerk of the District Court in Schiedam notified the OPK of that decision, adding that Sonja's true identity was known, that her parents had died in Germany, and that it was their wish that she be raised by van der Kaden and his wife. The court furthermore inquired if the OPK would object to a permanent custody arrangement for van der Kaden and his wife.

The second act of the custody proceedings started on September 14, 1945 when Fie Hartog testified before the OPK about Sonja's true identity and her own role in finding a foster family for Clara in 1942. Her deposition also stated that the van der Kadens had been called in by the civil registrar's office, presumably right after the war, and that they, following its recommendation, contacted the Schiedam district court judge. She said that "two friends (brothers) [likely Dolf and Jan Henkes] of the [birth] parents of the child stated that it was the father's wish that the child be raised in an ordinary Christian family, in case he and his wife would not return." This deposition was also made in front of a judge. Finally, she stated that the child was well taken care of, but that she would contact her biological cousins soon. With presumably no knowledge of her testimony, the Schiedam District Court Clerk informed the OPK on September 26, 1945 of its September 11 custody ruling. To which the OPK replied on October 10 that some of Sonja's birth relatives had survived and that the permanent custody ruling should be delayed. Between October 1945 and April 1946, more hearings were probably held. It is during that time that a detailed report was established. This OPK report indicates that the custody proceedings were not hostile:

They [the foster parents] do have a good relationship with relatives of the child who all greatly appreciate the couple and their love for the child and the loving atmosphere surrounding the child. The social setting of the foster parents is somewhat more modest than that of the parents, but that is, according to the relatives, only a minor difference, and is of no concern.

Regarding the issue of religion, the Commission wrote:

They [the biological parents] were not really immersed in church [synagogue] life and had many non-Jewish friends. They were raised in a Jewish environment but became somewhat detached (according to Mr. Landa and Mr. Laven). According to the ladies van Creveld, who clearly have a Jewish identity, the parents still felt Jewish. Hence, they feel that the statement about the child being raised in a Christian setting, can only be understood in the context of the recent events. However, in light of the parent's attitude and philosophy before these events, they have no grounds for wanting the child removed from her present environment.

And finally, about Clara's Jewish identity:

The child is a very charming five-year old little girl. She is calm, modest, and somewhat subdued. She is open and trusting toward the foster parents, and absolutely gives us the impression that she feels this to be her true home. The foster parents are comfortable with her presence. The child's appearance is typically Jewish, meaning that she would easily be recognized as such by the outside world. I mentioned to the foster parents that she should know her roots and that she should treasure those in her thoughts. They understood but the child is still too young to understand much of this.

The great-aunts Clara Drukker-van Creveld and Judith van Creveld, and great-uncle Karel Reens, who was married to great-aunt Esther van Creveld, signed affidavits on 28 January 1946 stating that they had no opposition to Sonja remaining in the care of the van der Kadens. The day after desisting, tante Juul wrote the OPK requesting that the Henkes family "should not have any say in the upbringing of the child." A great-aunt on Sonja's biological father's side, tante Sien born Spetter, and her husband Willem Adriaan Landa, appealed for a co-guardianship arrangement. The Commission received a letter from the Twentsche Bank in February 1946 stating that Willem Adriaan Landa had a good income as Director of N.V. Drop, but that the bank could not judge whether he would be suitable as guardian. The decision to keep the van der Kadens as temporary legal guardians stayed. This temporary situation lapsed *de facto* into a permanent one when the Commission stated that Clara van Thijn was no longer considered a war orphan. This, however, was stated in a letter but to the best of my knowledge never confirmed in official court documents.

The third act of the custody proceedings began in July 1946. A circular dated July 26, 1946 from the Commission Director reminded all foster parents of the Commission's sole jurisdiction over all war foster children. The circular was clearly intended to fend off custody claims by Jewish organizations and relatives. This episode sheds light on the van der Kaden's fear of losing Clara. On July 29, 1946, Willem van der Kaden visited the OPK office in a "highly indignant" state of mind. He had to be reassured by the Commission authorities that the circular in fact favored him. A few weeks later, on September 3, the van der Kadens officially registered as foster parents before the OPK. The Clerk of the Schiedam District Court wrote one last letter to the OPK on October 4, 1946, stating that no record of Clara van Thijn's birth place could be found, upon which the OPK replied on October 18, sending her birth certificate with the date of October 19, 1940. These are the last documents known, so the matter of the temporary custody seems to have been left standing. It is also during that time that monies came to the van der Kaden. The Inquiry Committee for Losses and Damages (Schade Enquête Commissie Rotterdam) began to handle compensation monies from Sara de Vries-van Creveld, Clara's grandmother.

A recently retrieved record from the district court in Schiedam for Clara van Thijn only shows two entries. The first entry from September 28, 1945 concerns the appointment of Willem van der Kaden as temporary guardian and Elisabeth Post as temporary co-guardian effective September 11, 1945. The second entry is dated January 24, 1956, appointing Pop's younger brother Hendrikus van der Kaden as co-guardian and removing Elisabeth van der Kaden-Post from that position. It is quite conceivable that this arrangement was made for the protection of Sonja in case something were to happen to her foster parents. It appears that Mom and Pop were never appointed permanent guardians.

Willy Vink befriended Sonja when she started second grade. "My mother told me that Sonja was a Jewish girl. She was found on the Boerhavenlaan where she was standing alone with a stuffed bear. The parents who lived nearby [the van der Kaden] had found and adopted her. Her parents had apparently been sent to a camp. I must NEVER NEVER talk to her about that. It could ruin her live, and I would not want to have that on my conscience." So strong was this admonition to "keep quiet to keep Sonja safe" that Willy did not break the silence until 1986. Another friend from the postwar years, Jacques Detiger, whose father was active in the Resistance and kept his neighborhood fed and secure during the war, was likewise admonished. Jacques remembers that the class knew that she was different, "she was dark," the students whispered; they were told to not ask about her looks and not talk about it. The excerpts of Willy's letters in the main text were pulled from an email exchange between Willy Vink and Alice-Catherine Carls in August 2014.

Alice van Gelder

One of Mau's maternal aunts, Roselina Spetter, and her husband Noach van Gelder, emigrated in early 1939 to the United States. Their daughter and Mau's cousin Alida (Alice) van Gelder, her husband Steven

(Shlomo) Shulster, and baby Jocelyn, wanted to leave for the United States too, but were delayed because Steven, having been born in a territory annexed by Poland after World War I, was not eligible for a US visa. They left the Netherlands in May 1940 on one of the last ships out of Rotterdam before the German invasion. They arrived in Curaçao and were granted entry into the USA thanks to Roselina's first cousin Isidore Spetter who, as comptroller for the Holland America Line and living in New York since 1911, arranged for their landing. By December 1940, they were safe at Alice's parents in New York. They resettled in Oakland, California in 1942, where their second daughter Beverly was born in 1948. Roselina and Noach eventually moved back to The Netherlands. Alice, Steven and their daughters' families moved to Israel.

Isidore Spetter

As comptroller with the Holland America Line, oom Isidore (Ies) Spetter played an important role in helping the Noach Spetter family, the van der Kadens, as well as tens of other Dutch families immigrate into the United States. He often arranged the necessary paperwork and assumed leadership positions in a variety of organizations aimed at bringing Dutch immigrant families closer together and building a community support structure. This included his chairing of the "New Netherlands' branch of Het Algemeen Nederlands Verbond. Isidore retired from the HAL in 1952 after 50 years of dedicated service, upon which he received a prestigious recognition from the Queen of the Netherlands and became *Ridder in the Orde van Oranje Nassau* (Knight of the Order of Orange-Nassau). Oom Ies, widowed and an American citizen, married his widowed cousin tante Sien Spetter in 1954. They eventually moved back to Barendrecht in The Netherlands. There he died in 1959.

Postwar Emigration

The reason behind the emigration of the van der Kaden family is not clear. Because the custody arrangement for Clara never became permanent, it is possible that the van der Kadens emigrated out of concern of losing her, or because they wanted to shield her from the grim past. In the early 1950's, children could still be removed from their foster families and placed under the custody of Jewish organizations if there were strong social or financial indicators that that would be in the best interest of the child. The van der Kadens were not alone, however, as thousands of families moved away from the old continent, hoping for a better future for them and their children. Other concerns included the rising tensions of the Cold War and the still bleak future of Europe.

The year 1952 was a peak year for postwar emigration from The Netherlands. Several factors contributed to the mass emigration. Rebuilding Holland went slower than expected and unemployment was looming. There was a general fear that the population was growing much too fast and that there would not be enough housing and employment. It would take a while before industry was rebuilt. Farm land became scarce. The general mood was pessimistic as The Netherlands had lost the Dutch Indies in 1949; Cold War fears were running high. The Dutch government actively promoted emigration by offering emigration subsidies and special courses, and made special arrangements with countries like Canada, Australia, and the US. Even though the US had immigration quotas, they mostly applied to other countries, not the western European countries. Most emigrants went to Canada. Australia was second and the US was third. The appeal of Canada was vast swaths of farm land. The appeal of the US was primarily its high standard of living. Compared to other European countries, Netherlands was second (behind Portugal) in the percentage of people emigrating after the war. The government even provided subsidies for emigration through consulting agencies. A poll taken in 1948 indicated that 1/3rd of the population considered emigrating. In the end, 3.5% left but this is still a very large number. By the early 1960's, emigration had dropped to normal levels.

Selected Bibliography

Memoirs and Auto-Biographies

Ernest H. Cassuto. *The last Jew of Rotterdam*. New Kensington, PA: Whitaker House (1974).

Karen Levine. *Hana's suitcase*. Park Ridge, IL: Albert Whitman & Co. (2002).

Josua Ossendrijver. *Verdoezeld verleden – kind van de oorlog*. Hilversum, Netherlands: Verbum Press (2014).

Philip Staal. *Settling the Account*. Bloomington, IN: iUniverse Press (2015).

Carry Ulreich. s Nachts droom ik van vrede. Zoetermeer, Netherlands: Mozaïek (2016).

Leon B. van Leeuwen. *Let my half cry*. Lincoln, NE: iUniverse Press (2007).

Monographs

Bert Jan Flim. *Saving the Children. History of the Organized Effort to Rescue Jewish Children in the Netherlands, 1942-1945*. Bethesda, MD: CDI Press (2005).

Jacob Presser. *Ashes in the Wind. The Destruction of Dutch Jewry*. London: Souvenir Press (2010).

Philip Staal. *Roestvrijstaal, een speurtocht naar de erfenis van Joodse oorlogswezen*. Delft, Netherlands: Eburon Press (2008).

Diana L. Wolfe. *Beyond Anne Frank: Hidden Children and Postwar Families in Holland*. University of California Press (2007).

Primary Sources

Archives of The Netherlands-North. http://noord-hollandsarchief.nl/

Belvédère House. http://www.belvedererotterdam.nl

Camp Westerbork. http://www.kampwesterbork.nl/en/

Commission for War Children (OPK).
    http://www.oorlogsgetroffenen.nl/

Digitized newspapers. http://delpher.nl

Jacqueline Phillips Interview.
    https://collections.ushmm.org/search/catalog/irn43341

National Archives of the Netherlands.
    https://www.nationaalarchief.nl/en

Sonja DuBois Interview.
    https://collections.ushmm.org/search/catalog/irn41499

Yad Vashem. https://www.yadvashem.org

General Sources

Bombing of Rotterdam.
    http://brandgrens.nl/bombardement-en-brandgrens

Dutch Jewry genealogy. https://www.dutchjewry.org

Dutch Registry. https://www.wiewaswie.nl/

Genealogy. http://www.ancestry.com

Het verhaal van Sifra.
    http://www.belvedererotterdam.nl/downlads/sifra/

Jewish genealogy. https://www.jewishgen.org

Jews of Rotterdam. http://joodserfgoedrotterdam.nl

Loods 24. http://www.loods24rotterdam.nl

Monument to the Jews of Rotterdam. http://www.joodsmonument.nl

Netherlands during WW II. https://www.verzetsmuseum.org; also see: http://www.niod.nl

Schifrah, an Ode to life.
     http://www.belvedererotterdam.nl/downloads/schifrah/

Contributor's Biographies

Sonja DuBois

Born in Rotterdam on October 19, 1940, Sonja DuBois became a Holocaust child survivor when her parents were deported to Auschwitz in July 1942. She was raised by a Dutch foster family first in Rotterdam, then in the United States without fully being told about her biological family and her true identity. Her lifelong search for understanding has led her to be a witness for the impact of the Holocaust. She has spoken to hundreds of students and general audiences in Tennessee and Kentucky. She has been featured in the Tennessee Holocaust Commission's *Living On* exhibit. She donated artifacts to the United States Holocaust Memorial Museum in Washington, DC, which has a recorded interview of her life. She participated in the 70th anniversary commemorations of the end of World War II in Rotterdam. She lives in Knoxville, Tennessee, with her husband Ron, her best friend, whom she married in 1962. They have two daughters, five grand-children, and two great-grand-children.

Alice-Catherine Carls

Alice-Catherine Carls (1950) is Tom Elam Distinguished Professor of History at the University of Tennessee at Martin. She is a diplomatic and cultural historian of 20th century Europe. Her monographs include a study of the Free City of Danzig in 1938-1939 (Ossolineum, Poland, 1982) and *Europe from War to War, 1914-1945* (Routledge, 2018), co-authored with husband Stephen D. Carls. As a translator, she has published several volumes of Polish and English poetry and prose into French. She is serving on the editorial board of several journals in the United States and abroad, and on the jury of the Paris-based "Cénacle Européen des Arts, Lettres, et Poésie. She currently finishing a 4-year appointment to the Tennessee Great War Commission.

Hanno H. Weitering

Hanno H. Weitering (1962) is a native of Rotterdam, The Netherlands. He obtained a PhD in mathematics and natural sciences from the University of Groningen in 1991 and emigrated to the United States shortly thereafter. He is a professor of physics and department chair at the University of Tennessee, Knoxville, and a Fellow of the American Physical Society. He authored numerous original research papers in professional physics journals and has led many federally funded research projects. He has a keen interest in World War II history and contributed to *Finding Schifrah* primarily through research and translation of Dutch historical documents.